Befriending the Stranger

Jean Vanier

Befriending the Stranger

Paulist Press
New York/Mahwah, NJ

Design and produced by Sandie Boccacci

Cover and interior images are from *La Cappella Redemptoris Mater del Papa Giovanni Paolo II* [The Redemptoris Mater Chapel of Pope John Paul II], edited by Apa–Clement–Valenziano, and are reprinted here with the kind permission and cooperation of Libreria Editrice Vaticana.

First published as *La source des larnes* by Editions Parole et Silence
First published in English in Canada by Novalis.

A catalogue record for this book is available from the Library of Congress.
Library of Congress Control Number: 2009942815

ISBN: 978-0-8091-4690-1

Published in the United States of America in 2010 by
Paulist Press
997 Macarthur Boulevard
Mahwah, New Jersey, 07430
United States of America

www.paulistpress.com

Printed and bound in Canada

Contents

CONTENTS

Preface

In the communities of l'Arche we live and journey together, men and women with disabilities and those who feel called to share their lives with them. We are all learning the pain and joy of community life, where the weakest members open hearts to compassion and lead us into a deeper union with Jesus. We are learning to befriend them, and through and with them, to befriend Jesus.

Our communities, like those of Faith and Light, are founded on a belief in the value of each person no matter what their culture, religion, abilities or disabilities. We are all called to grow in love, wisdom and the acceptance of others. Some of our communities are rooted in the Catholic faith; some have become ecumenical; we live the joys of unity and the pain of divisions. We grow together in trying to live the message of Jesus.

Originally this text was *spoken*. They were talks I gave at a retreat in the Dominican Republic for people immersed in the daily life of l'Arche in Latin America and in the Caribbean. These "assistants", as they are called in l'Arche, need to be refreshed and renewed. Our lives can sometimes be stressful as we live with people carrying anguish. We all need to deepen our love for Jesus, hidden in those who are often unwanted. On the last day of the retreat, many of the assistants, in response to a call of God, announced their bonding or "covenant" with Jesus and with all the members of their community, especially the weakest and poorest. Later these talks were put into book form, keeping the style of the retreat – six days put into six chapters. Each talk is a step on a journey of faith and of love. Each should be read as such: quietly, peacefully, so that the reader may be drawn more deeply into the mystery of God's love revealed in Jesus.

Although this week of reflection and prayer was for people committed to l'Arche, it is also for all those who are searching to live the gospel. It is for those who believe that the renewal of the Church and the unity of the followers of Jesus will come as we serve and befriend those who appear to us as "strange", "different", the unwanted and the lonely of our societies and as we learn to befriend our own poverty, the "strange" and the lonely within us. I would like to make mine the words of Cardinal Etchegary during his talk to young people in Rome for the new millennium:

> The church is asking you to be attentive to the weak and the vulnerable, those in whom Jesus Christ rejoices because they see what has been hidden to the clever and the capable (cf Mt 11:25). Never forget this criteria, it is the most precious, the most certain, the most concrete criteria which will help you to recognize what Christ expects from you ... The direction is clear: live poorly as Christ did, live with the poor in order to live with Christ. The renewal of the church always comes as we dare to live a covenant with the poor.

JEAN VANIER
L'Arche, Trosly

INTRODUCTION: *Jesus wept*

As Jesus drew near to Jerusalem, he wept.
The mysterious tears of Jesus.
He could foresee what was going to happen.
He knew that Jerusalem would be destroyed,
that the "Holy City" would become the "city of pain",
the "city of war and conflict".
Jesus wept:

> **"If you had only understood the message of peace ..."**
>
> (cf. Lk 19:42)

But we do not understand the message of peace.
We so often ignore the heart of the gospel message.

Jesus weeps over our world today.
He weeps over our countries where inequality, division, exclusion
    are so dominant.
As we look more deeply into the gospel message
    and the gift of l'Arche
we will touch the mystery of Jesus weeping.
In our l'Arche communities we welcome people who had been
    rejected, put away.
They have wept many tears.
L'Arche has been built on their tears.

Luisito is a man with severe disabilities.
Before his welcome in l'Arche, in Santo Domingo,
    he used to live in the street
in a small hut near the Catholic church.

When his mother died, he was left all alone.
From time to time the neighbours would give him something to
    eat,
but no one was really committed to him:
he was dirty and smelly; his body was twisted;
    he could not walk, nor talk.
People found it difficult to look at him; he disturbed them.
Yet today he is one of the founding members of l'Arche in Santo
    Domingo
and it is wonderful to see him in the community.

Claudia came to l'Arche in Suyapa (in Honduras) from San Felipe
    Asylum.
Blind and autistic, she had been abandoned as a child.
During her first year in the l'Arche community, "Casa Nazaret",
she was quite disturbed and anguished;
she screamed a lot.
Now she is more peaceful.
She sets the table, works in the workshop ...
When I visited the community some time ago, I found her
    walking around in the yard,
smiling and singing to herself.
I asked her if I could ask her a question: "Si [yes], Juan," she replied.
"Claudia, why are you so happy?"
"Dios [God]," she replied.
This young girl who had been abandoned, whom no one had
    wanted,
had become a friend of God.

We are privileged, wherever we may be,
no matter what our place in society,
to be close to the Luisitos and Claudias around us,
in our families, in neighbourhoods and in our communities.
Being close to them, we are close to Jesus.
That is the mystery, the secret of the gospel of Jesus:
Luisito renders Jesus present!

It seems foolish to say that.
Much that I say may well seem quite foolish
because the gospel is truly a message of folly.
It is so simple, so amazing, that it is difficult to believe it is true,
just as it must have been difficult for Mary to believe
that the little one she was carrying in her womb
  and later in her arms,
   was God!
This little child needed her to feed him, to take care of him
but even more needed her to love him.
A child needs to be loved.
The "Word-made-flesh", Jesus, needed to be loved.

It is difficult for us to believe in a God who is so humble and
  vulnerable.
Isn't God first and foremost the All-Powerful One,
  Creator of heaven and earth,
Creator of the whole world of plants, fish, animals,
Creator of man and of woman?
God is so great!
When we look at the stars,
  the distance between the stars and our planet,
when we imagine the suns behind the suns,
  the galaxies behind the galaxies,
we become aware of the greatness of God.
Yet this same God became flesh, became a little child.

In John's Gospel, Philip says to Jesus:

> **"Lord, show us the Father and we shall be satisfied."**

Jesus replies:

> **"Have I been with you so long and yet you do not know me,
> Philip? Whoever has seen me has seen the Father ..."** (14:9)

Whoever sees Jesus, sees God.

Whoever touches Jesus, touches God.
When Mary carried the baby Jesus in her arms,
   she was carrying God in her arms.
This is the folly of the Incarnation which Jesus extends even
   further when he says:

> **"Whatever you did to one of the least of these my brethren,
> you did it to me."** (Matt 25:40)

Whoever visits a prisoner, clothes the naked, welcomes a stranger
is visiting, clothing and welcoming God. This is a great mystery!

In order to enter into the mystery of the gospel
we need to be open and attentive.
   We need to listen with our whole being.
What we are going to hear is in fact too much for us to understand,
unless the Holy Spirit helps us,
   the only one who can truly teach us,
the only one who can enlighten any of my words.
It is with the help of the Holy Spirit that our hearts can be opened,
   touched and nourished.

It may be important to listen to my words
but it is even more important to be attentive to the Word of God
as it is revealed in each one of us.
Let us listen carefully to the gospel message,
   to the folly of God's message
and to the Spirit of Jesus who dwells in each of us.

God spoke through the words of the prophet Hosea:

> **"Therefore, behold, I will allure her
> and bring her into the wilderness,
> and speak tenderly to her."** (Hos 2:14)

We may not be in the wilderness,
but we have all come away from our daily lives and activities.
For some of us, this time of reflection may feel desert-like.
That is a sign that Jesus is calling us, leading us, drawing us
so that he can speak gently to us, heart to heart.
Jesus speaks not only to our heads, to our intelligence,
he speaks also to our hearts, to our deepest selves.
So let us open our hearts with trust
    and receive all that he wants to give us.

The prophet continued:

> **"I will give her back her vineyards ..."**

which means I will show her how fruitful her life is,

> **"and make the Valley of Achor a door of hope."**

Yes, our lives are called to bear much fruit
because Jesus wants us to give life to others.
We find it difficult to give life,
    to hold and carry people in their weakness.
We are often frightened of reality because reality can be painful
and a source of disappointment.
We tend to escape into a world of illusions
    and to seek refuge in dreams.
We bury ourselves in ideas and theories
    or fill our days with distractions.
A survey in the United States showed that people watch television
    twenty-eight to thirty-two hours a week!
The television screen has taken over from reality.
We run away from our "Valley of Achor"
which is the place of our greatest and most intimate pain.
Yet that is the very place that God calls us to enter
so that it may be transformed into a door of hope.

The Valley of Achor was situated near Jericho.
It was a dangerous place, filled with snakes, scorpions
 and all kinds of wild beasts;
it was a place of fear that people tried to avoid.
Yet God declares that this valley of misfortune
 will become a door of hope.
What a mystery; a mystery filled with hope!

There is a "Valley of Achor" in each one of us:
for each of us there are events or hurts we do not want to
 remember, look at or come close to;
there are people and experiences that we try to avoid
because they bring up too much pain in us
and we are frightened of pain.
Certain people disturb us; they are "strange", "different";
we cannot bear their pain or the pain they evoke in us.
Yet God tells us that if we enter into these places of pain and
 welcome these people
they will become for us a "door of hope".
If we become close to the people our societies reject,
 exclude and crush,
people who are hidden away in asylums,
we will discover that they can become a "door of hope".
So too if we accept the things inside our own selves that we reject:
the blockages, the bitterness, the fears,
all that we may be ashamed of;
if we dare to penetrate into our inner "Valley of Achor"
it will indeed become a door of hope for us.

But we cannot do it all alone.
We need to walk hand in hand with Jesus,
to let him guide us
and reveal to us the heart of the gospel.

DAY ONE

"I want to stay in your home today"
(Luke 19)

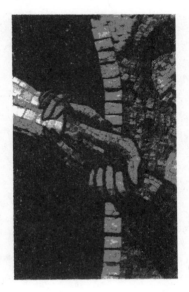

God is calling us into the world of love

Jesus looks at our world today,
at our big cities, our countries
with all their divisions, inequality, hatred, and violence
and he weeps.

Jesus came into the world to bring peace,
to bring all people together into one body
  wherein each person has a place.
But we human beings have turned our world into a place
  of competition, rivalry, conflict and war
  between races, religions, social classes and countries.
The world has become a place in which each person feels they
  have to protect and defend themselves, their own family, their
  own country, their own class, their own religion.
Nuclear weapons, missiles and machine guns
  are the outer, visible signs
of our inner, invisible, personal weapons.
These we bring out as soon as we feel threatened, humiliated and
  rejected,
or when we feel we are not given our rightful space;
  our rightful place.
Violence and hatred exist today just as they are described in the
  Book of Genesis:

> **The Lord saw that the wickedness of humankind was great on
> the earth ... (6:5)**

> **Now the earth was corrupt in God's sight and the earth was
> filled with violence. (6:11)**

The same violence and corruption fill the earth today.
The same process of hatred and division repeats itself
  over and over again,

day after day, year after year,
nourished by the fear and vulnerability of the human heart.
For if we human beings are violent,
  it is mainly because we are so vulnerable.
Violence is a response to a wounded heart
when it feels misunderstood, rejected, unloved.
As soon as we feel the slightest rejection,
the wound reopens and our defence mechanisms rise up.

I remember my visit to a top security prison in Kingston, Ontario.
I told the prisoners about the men and women we have welcomed
    in l'Arche
— their pain, their sense of failure and rejection, their depression,
sometimes even their self-mutilation.
I spoke about their broken childhood.
As I shared these stories about our people in l'Arche
I knew that I was in fact telling them their own story,
the story of their lives, their experience of rejection, grief,
    insecurity, and failure.
At the end of my talk one of the inmates got up and screamed at me:
"You," he said, "you've had an easy life!
You do not understand what we are living!
When I was four years old, I saw my mother raped
    right in front of me!
When I was seven, I was sold by my father for sex.
When I was thirteen the 'men in blue' (the police) came to get me.
If anyone else comes into this prison to talk about love
I will kick his bloody head in!"

I listened to him but did not know what to say or do.
It was as if he had me against a wall.
I prayed
and then I said: "It's true what you say. I have had an easy life!
It's true, I do not know what you have lived.
But what I do know is
    that everything you have just said is important.

People outside this prison often judge you
    without knowing your pain,
your story, your childhood experiences.
Will you allow me to tell people outside
    what you have just told me today?"
He replied "Yes".
Then I added, "You may have things to tell us,
but one day you will be getting out of prison
and perhaps you will need to know and hear things about life
    outside the prison."
I asked him if I could come back when I was in the region.
And he replied "Yes".

When the question time was over
I went up to this man and I shook his hand.
I asked him his name and where he came from.
Then I was inspired to ask him whether he was married
and when he said "Yes" I asked him to tell me about his wife.
This man who had been so violent
who had seemed to have such hatred in him,
broke down in tears.
He told me about his wife, who was in Montreal,
    in a wheelchair.
He had not seen her for two years!
I was in front of a wounded, vulnerable little child,
weeping, crying out for love and tenderness.
My talk about our need for love, communion of hearts and
    gentleness
– everything he had been deprived of –
had reopened the deep wound in his heart
and he had found it unbearable!

He taught me something important:
the source of our tears and violence often lies much deeper than
    arrogance and selfishness.

Tears and violence can be ways of protecting ourselves
    from what is unbearable,
from our own vulnerability
from our fear of pain.

In the midst of all the violence and corruption of the world
God invites us today to create new places of belonging,
places of sharing, of peace and of kindness,
places where no-one needs to defend himself or herself;
places where each one is loved and accepted with one's own
    fragility, abilities and disabilities.
This is my vision for our churches:
    that they become places of belonging, places of sharing.

We see that sometimes our churches, our Christian communities,
are filled with the same power struggles,
the same story of divisions and conflict
because our churches, like our communities,
are made up of broken, wounded men and women,
    like you and like me.
Constantly we need to be led back
    to the essential message of Jesus,
the message of love, the message of the beatitudes and of humility.
We have to become increasingly aware of the many different ways
    we can create division,
the ways in which we criticise others;
our need to prove that we are better than others.

The Second Vatican Council was called by Pope John XXIII
    in the 1960s.
It was a time of great renewal for the Roman Catholic Church.
It reminded church leaders of the importance of simplicity:
Jesus did not teach his disciples
    to become the "princes" of the Church
but rather to wash each other's feet.
During the colonisation of the Americas,

some Christian colonisers questioned whether or not
  native people were fully human.
Theologians wondered whether or not a slave had a soul.
It took time for slavery to be condemned by the Church.
Does this not show how far we have all strayed from the original
  message of Jesus?

The Letter of James, written shortly after the death of Jesus,
tells us how quickly the community of believers had changed:
people were paying more attention to those dressed in fine clothes
whilst keeping those more shabbily dressed at the back of the
  assembly (cf. 2:4–9) ...
James was hurt and angry.
Hadn't Jesus died because he had put the poor and the weak at the
  heart of the community?
And now this same community of followers of Jesus
  was gradually excluding them!

With each new era, each new situation of poverty and oppression,
God calls people forth in a new way;
God's call is ever new and yet ever the same.
When the waters filled and engulfed the earth,
we see how God called forth Noah,

    a righteous man,
    blameless in his generation and who walked with God.
                                      (Gen. 6:9)

As we become more aware of the violence and corruption
  that fill our world
we too become aware of God's call to us
to welcome those who are weak, crushed and oppressed.

God calls us to grow in love,
  each one with his/her specific vocation.
Too often the word "vocation" has been attributed only to people

who are religious sisters or brothers or ordained: ministers or priests.
Doesn't each one of us have a vocation, a call, from God?
Isn't marriage a real vocation?
Do not couples need a new gift from God in order to be able to
    live fully their married life?
Is that not why we need to receive blessings,
    to receive the sacraments;
an affirmation of our commitment, in front of others?
Do not people with disabilities have a special vocation?
Paul reminds us of their call with great force:

> Consider your call ...
> God chose what is foolish in the world to shame the wise;
> God chose what is weak in the world to shame the strong;
> God chose what is low and despised in the world ...
>
> (1 Cor 1:26, 27–8)

It is important to pray for vocations, for *all* vocations!
Just as God called forth Noah,
    God is calling each one of us in our own way
to help build "an Ark", a community of love
wherein love conquers hatred,
inclusion conquers exclusion,
unity conquers division.
Let us ask Jesus to help us hear his call within each of our hearts.

Recognising our call

God calls forth men and women in every age ... and in our own
    times too.
We should not think that we are too insignificant, too unimportant
    or unworthy
to be called by God.
God does not choose the strong, the most influential
    and the most learned,
but rather the weak, the humble, the most needy ...

Throughout the Scriptures God's choice remains constant.
Look at the story of David and the way he was chosen to be king
    (cf. 1 Sam 16:1–13).
The Lord sent Samuel
    to choose and consecrate one of the sons of Jesse as king.
Jesse presented to Samuel his seven sons,
all were tall, strong, bright young men.
The Lord did not choose any of them
but inspired Samuel to ask Jesse if there were any others.
Jesse replied:

> "There remains the youngest but behold, he is keeping the
> sheep." ...
> Samuel took the horn of oil and anointed him in the midst of
> his brothers.

The prophet Jeremiah did not know how to speak.
Moses stuttered.
It is difficult to be a leader or a prophet when you cannot speak
    or when you stutter!
Look at Mary of Magdala, who was caught up in prostitution.
Jesus loved her, called her
and gave her an important and unique place in the gospel.

Then there is the story of the Samaritan woman (cf. Jn 4),
the only person in the whole of the gospels
    to whom Jesus personally revealed that he was the Messiah.
In front of others he had performed miracles
    and proclaimed the Word of God
but never had he said openly to anyone that he was the Messiah.
It was the Father who revealed to the hearts of Peter and the
    disciples
that Jesus was the Christ, the Anointed One.
And this Samaritan woman who received
    this revelation from Jesus himself
was not even Jewish.

She belonged to a group that was considered by the Jewish people
   to be a sect
because they had broken away from Jewish tradition.
Moreover, this woman was not only rejected by the Jews
but was rejected and marginalised by her own people
because of her way of living:
she had lived with five different men
and the man she was now living with was not her husband.
The woman from Samaria was a very wounded, broken woman,
   filled with guilt.
She did not know how to live a committed relationship of love
because, fundamentally, she did not know
   that she herself was loved.
She probably felt that God rejected her
   just as the others rejected her.

At one point this wounded, broken woman says to Jesus:

> **"I know that the Messiah is coming (the one who is called
> Christ) and when he comes, he will show us all things."**
> Jesus said to her: **"I who speak to you am he."** (Jn 4:25–6)

God's ways are not our ways; God's choices are not the choices of
   society.
God chooses "the poor, the weak, the needy",
those who recognise their poverty –
not just a material poverty but an inability to cope with life,
a feeling of powerlessness and not knowing what to do.
A mother who has just lost a child is "poor".
A woman whose husband has left her is "poor".
A man who has lost his job is "poor".
The girl who learns she has cancer is "poor".
The man who senses his body growing older and weaker is "poor".
People who are faced with difficult family situations are "poor".
The problem is that we refuse to admit our weakness, our needs,
   our poverty

because we are frightened of rejection.
We have been taught to be strong, to be "the best", to win
    in order to become "someone".
Since society tends to marginalise those who are weak
we think that weakness means rejection.
So we try to hide our poverty for as long as we can
and to pretend that we are strong;
we build up an appearance of being in control.

We need to hear that gentle, inner voice of God who tells us:
    "You do not need to pretend.
    You do not need to hide your weakness.
    You can be yourself.
    I didn't call you to l'Arche or to another form of community
    first of all to help others
    or to prove that you were generous or efficient.
    I called you because you are poor,
    just like the ones you came to serve,
    and because the Kingdom of God is promised to the poor."

God calls each one of us.
There are many reasons why we go to a church or a group
but we only remain committed
if we realise that we are there because God has called us.
We will continually be disappointed or discouraged
when we encounter the fragility of people in the community
and our own fragility
unless we discover that if we have become members of a
    community
it is because God has called us to serve in that way.
Our belonging, our commitment, is a response to a call from God.

It is the vocation of the Claudias and Luisitos of our communities,
who are at the heart of our community life;
it is the vocation of the assistants called to be full time in the houses;
it is the vocation of families, pastoral ministers and board members

who give support.
Whatever our role in the community,
we will not really understand our place and put down roots
until we realise that we are answering a call from Jesus
who invites us into a mysterious path of growth
    in love and compassion.
Let us ask Jesus to help us discover our poverty,
not to be frightened or ashamed of it
and to become more aware of our call, our mission.

Rooted in faithfulness

God's call is different for each one of us
and yet it is the same.
It is a call to grow in love, in wisdom and in inner freedom,
and thus to bring greater love, peace and freedom into the world.
Once we have recognised our call and found our place –
    which takes time –
then we need to learn to put down roots
    and to be faithful to that call.

Each person has his/her role in building the community.
Each has to deepen his/her sense of being called.
It takes time for choices to deepen, to mature and to bear fruit.
Each call is unique
but we are *all* called to give life
    and to give life *together*, as a community.

Mark's Gospel tells us the story of a young man who ran up to
    Jesus and knelt before him:

> **"Good Teacher, what must I do to inherit eternal life?"**

Jesus told him about the commandments of God,
to which the man replied that he had kept them all from his youth.
Then Mark tells us:

"Jesus looked at him and loved him".

Imagine the expression in Jesus' eyes
    as he looked at this man and loved him.
Then he said:

> "You lack one thing; go, sell what you have,
>   and give to the poor, and you will have a treasure in heaven;
>   and come, follow me." (10:17–22)

He was saying: "Come and be with me. We will walk together;
    we shall be friends.
      I will teach you how to be gentle, kind and loving
      in the midst of a world of violence and self-centredness.
      I will show you how to become a man or woman of peace,
      a man or woman of hope.
      Do not be afraid, I will show you how to live
      so that your whole life, your whole being,
      becomes a sign of the Good News."
Mark tells us that this young man became frightened and turned
    away from Jesus.

When we discover and welcome God's call,
    something beautiful happens in us:
we experience the love of God for us
and a whole new world opens up inside us.
We also realise that it is a very demanding call.
We are invited to leave our former, familiar world,
and let go of what we used to know and hold on to;
all this implies loss.
We receive something new
but at the same time we must let go of something else.
When a woman decides to marry a man,
she is saying no to thousands of others!
When someone is called to a long-term commitment in l'Arche
that means that she has to let go of her former way of living,

the freedom to do what she wants with her day, with her friends,
etc.

Grief and loss are inseparable from the call.
If we accept the call but not the loss
    we will live in a contradiction.
When people make a decision, for example to live in l'Arche,
but do not fully accept the consequences of their decision,
    it is a cause of great distress.
They constantly feel sorry for themselves,
sorry that they do not have a higher salary,
    or more time for themselves,
shorter working hours, etc.

There is the call
and there is the loss.
But who wants loss?
When I left the navy more than fifty years ago,
    I sold everything I had,
which wasn't much, and gave it to the poor.
Today I do not have much to sell
    and I doubt if anyone would want what I have!
But the call and the loss continue.
Today I am called to let go of other things: attitudes, fears,
    prejudices, security, certitudes,
the need to be in control ...
There is a daily "letting go"
because each day Jesus is calling me
    to become more loving, more compassionate,
more present to people,
more fully a child of God, more free from fear.

In Luke's Gospel there is another story of a call.
It is the story of Zacchaeus (19:1–10).
Zacchaeus was a man who suffered from being
    so small in stature that

whenever he was in a crowd, he was unable to see
    even if he stood on tiptoes.
That was not his only problem.
He was also a rich tax collector,
a job that made him quite unpopular with other "true" Jews.
Tax collectors collected taxes *from* the Jewish population
    for the Roman occupiers.
They were considered collaborators, even traitors,
and in fact they were benefiting from the Roman occupation;
often extracting more money than was required
    in order to put it into their own pockets.
So here was Zacchaeus, a rich tax collector and a collaborator with
    the Romans,
distrusted if not despised by his fellow Jews,
who had heard that Jesus was coming
    and who sought to see who this Jesus was.
But Zacchaeus could not see because of the crowd

      so he ran on ahead and climbed up into a sycamore tree to
      see him.

That must have made Jesus smile.
Imagine such an important man, the chief tax collector,
    perched in a tree!
Jesus looked up and said to him,

      "Zacchaeus, make haste and come down
      for I want to stay in your house today!"

Zacchaeus must have been surprised
and his wife probably did not believe him when he told her.
She may even have been furious; neither she nor the house was
    prepared for such a visit!
The house was perhaps untidy, the children dirty,
    the dinner not ready!
And you can imagine the surprise and anger
    amongst the religious authorities of Jericho

who thought that *they* were the ones Jesus should have honoured
    by his visit!
They were hurt and shocked by Jesus' choice
    to go to the house of a traitor.
The world was turned upside down.
Jesus so often acts in this way.
He turns our world of self-importance, honour
    and conventional virtues upside down.
He disturbs the established order of things and replaces it with a
    new order.
So Jesus went to Zacchaeus' home.
He did not tell him to sell all he had and to follow him.
Jesus said:

> **"I want to stay in your home today."**

To the rich young man Jesus says:
"Go, sell all you have, give the money to the poor and come follow me!"
To Zacchaeus Jesus says: **"I must stay in your home today."**
Both requests are demanding;
neither is easy to live out.
People often prefer to keep Jesus in the churches
    and places of worship,
where they can go and see him from time to time,
when they feel like it or when they feel the need.
But to have Jesus in their home –
    which is also the home of their hearts –
this is harder to accept!

When we welcome Jesus into our "home",
he transforms us and he transforms our way of living.
We know that people can be together in the same house,
existing but not sharing.
There is a kind of modus vivendi
which in fact helps them not to meet

but instead to avoid one another.
Women can be so taken up with their own occupations
    in the house or with friends;
men can hide behind their newspapers, the television or their
    problems at work.
Jesus tells the good homemaker
    to stop putting everything in order,
to sit down and listen to her children,
to *spend time* with them.
Jesus is telling the man, the typical workaholic,
that his first priority is not the television but his wife and children.
Sometimes men do not really know what it means to be a father.
They think that it is sufficient to provide for the material well-
    being of their children
and to tell them what he wants them to do with their lives.
A father is more than that:
to be a father means to love one's children, to listen to them,
to respect them and to foster their growth,
to protect them,
to trust them and to trust their intuitions,
to help them to find their own space.
Fatherhood, like motherhood, is a very beautiful vocation
    but a demanding one.
It is a call from God who wants to come and "stay in our home".

Let us take quiet time to listen to God's call,
To hear God call us by our name.
Let us rediscover our first love,
re-live our first call, our first "yes" to Jesus
or perhaps hear for the first time Jesus' call to follow him,
to love him,
to welcome him "into our home", into our hearts.

DAY TWO

*"You are precious in my eyes and honoured
and I love you"*

(Isaiah 43:4)

We are loved by God

The Lord spoke through the prophet Hosea:

> **"I will allure her, bring her into the wilderness
> and speak to her heart."** (Hos 2:14)

The wilderness can be frightening because we feel so alone,
away from our usual security,
　　our friends, our activities, our projects.
We feel powerless, as if left in a void.
But it is precisely there, in that place of poverty,
that God meets us and speaks to our hearts.
The Book of Hosea continues:

> **"And there she will answer as in the days of her youth
> as at the time when she came out of the land of Egypt."** (2:15)

For a while married couples remember the joy
of their engagement, their wedding, the honeymoon
but as the years go by and routine sets in they often forget.
We remember our first encounter with Jesus
　　which remains present in us for a while,
but then we forget.
People often remember the joy of their first contact with l'Arche,
but with time and daily tasks, they forget.
As the years go by, we become jaded
　　and everything seems a bit more grey.
But the Lord says:
　　"And there she will answer as in the days of her youth."
In other words:
"You will remember the taste of joy you experienced when you
　　were young" ...

We can imagine the Israelites' joy when,
  after all those years of slavery in Egypt,
they saw the sea opening up in front of them.
Suddenly they realised that they were truly free,
  liberated from the yoke of slavery!
Even greater than the joy of their liberation
was the joy of realising that all along the way
  God had been watching over them,
guiding them, leading them.
They were truly the people of God.
We have all had similar experiences
when we have felt that we were in an impossible situation,
  facing a brick wall;
all of a sudden there was a breakthrough.
We are not quite sure how it happened but it did.
We are free to go on, to move ahead.
In the network of l'Arche, 10 to 20 per cent of the communities
are usually in crisis at the same moment!
Communities go through times of tension, conflict
  and breakdowns.
When we get through the crisis, we rejoice and give thanks
but later on we can so easily forget how we were saved.
The Israelites forgot the way in which they had been liberated.
When water and food became scarce
and the road ahead of them seemed impossible,
they lost their certitude that God was guiding them
and they started to grumble, to doubt and to complain.
We too in l'Arche, when faced with apparently impossible situations,
can start to grumble, to doubt and to complain.
Yet we know that **"for God, nothing is impossible"**.
Crises constantly arise
as if they are necessary
  in order to make us turn back to God and to cry out for help.
Then God brings us back to the joys of the beginnings
and the certitude of God's faithful presence,
  guiding us, walking with us.

That is why the Lord says:

> "For I will remove the names of Ba'als from her mouth"
>
> (Hos 2:17)

which means,
"I will take away all those things that have become idols for you,
the things that you worship in place of God:
things that have taken on too much importance,
such as money, efficiency, know-how, reputation,
    even friendship and community.
You have put your trust in them instead of in me."

And the Lord continues, through Hosea:

> "And I will make for you on that day a covenant with the
> beasts of the field,
> the birds of the air and the creeping things of the ground;
> and I will abolish the bow, the sword and war from the land;
> and I will make you lie down in safety." (Hos 2:18)

We discover or re-discover the beauty and the depths
    of the Covenant
between God and each one of us:
the realisation that we are loved and protected,
that we are children of God
and that God has given us a promise of peace.
Our world seems very far from this vision of Hosea
but in our communities and families
    we can live and work together
so that there is no more rivalry, no more competition, no more
war.
We can try to build places where swords and bows are abolished,
places where each person works for the good of the whole.
It is beautiful to see families and communities
    that have become like one body
where each member is loved and respected for who they are.

"I will betroth you to me for ever;
I will betroth you to me in righteousness and in justice,
in steadfast love, and in mercy.
I will betroth you to me in faithfulness;
and you shall know the Lord." (Hos 2:19–20)

This is the final promise of God which began with
"I will allure her into the wilderness"
and ends in a betrothal, a covenant, in union with God.

"You shall know the Lord" is not some intellectual knowing
but the knowing that comes from a personal experience
    of God's presence,
an intimate presence such as between a husband and wife.
To know God is to live in God and to let God live in us
so that our hearts beat in unison,
so that we have the same desires, the same yearnings,
    the same priorities as God.
This personal experience of the love of God for ourselves
gives us a new inner strength;
this is the presence of the Holy Spirit
    dwelling in us and working through us.

I remember a letter I received from a girl who told me
that she had never sensed that she had been loved.
During her childhood she had the impression
    that her conception had been an error.
Nobody really wanted her.
Her parents used to talk with pride about her sister or brother
    but never about her;
it was as if she didn't exist.
She did not have any friends at school.
All this created a permanent wound in her
    that stayed with her throughout her young life.
She was convinced that no man could ever love her or want her.
Her letter continued:

"One day I was walking in the forest and I sat down under a tree
and suddenly I was filled with the certitude that I was loved by
   God."
Something rose up within her;
she realised that she was precious, important in the eyes of God.
It was a powerful experience that changed everything in her life:
and yet nothing was changed.
It is important to realise that our experience of God's love changes
   our whole life,
and yet nothing changes:
we remain the fruit of our past life,
the sum total of everything we have lived
   from the moment of our conception.
Each person, each event is deeply engraved in our being;
even if our memory does not recall, our body remembers.

Our body, our whole being, carries within it the marks
of each act of gentleness and tenderness
but also each wound, each sense of rejection,
each word or gesture which gave us the impression
   that we were loved or not loved
or that we were guilty.
This sense of guilt is hidden deeply within us all.
The very first time a child feels rejection,
   the heart of the child is wounded
— perhaps simply because no one listens to her
or because her mother is tired or too busy with the other children;
the child does not understand.
From that wound is born the sense of not being loved,
and thus the feeling of not being loveable.
If the child is rejected, it is because she is guilty; she is no good.
This sense of guilt can paralyse us interiorly,
   destroy our self-confidence
and give birth to doubt and to mistrust of self and of others.
It can govern our lives and actions even if we do not realise it.

Our lives are moulded and fashioned
    by all the graces we have received or refused;
by all the gestures of love as well as the acts of hatred or
    indifference;
by our successes as well as our failures.
Absolutely everything is engraved in our being.
So the experience of being loved by God
    does not change our lives completely,
yet something is changed
    when we realise that God loves us just as we are,
not as we would like to be
nor as our parents or society would have liked us to be.
God loves us *today*
with our gifts, our qualities, as well as our failures and our fragility.
If we have the impression that other people are disappointed in us
because we do not live up to their expectations;
if there seems to be a gap
    between the way in which others perceive us
    and who we really are,
between what we like to think we can do
    and what we can actually do,
we need to discover that God is never disappointed in us.
God knows us;
God knows our abilities and disabilities;
God knows that we are a mixture of light and darkness.
Others may be disappointed
    because they have an ideal image of Him
but not God, who knows me today just as I am.
God does not live in the past or in the future
but in the "now" of the present moment.
God sees me in my present reality as I am in each present moment.

I gave a talk a few years ago to a group of religious sisters
    in the United Kingdom.
One of the sisters kept interrupting me during my talks
which annoyed me. It annoyed the other sisters even more.

At the end of my talk, she asked to see me.
She told me: "You know, I'm a difficult person."
(I had already noticed that!)
And she added: "No man could ever have chosen me."
(I had thought that too!)
"But," she continued, "God has chosen me
    with all that I am, just as I am."
Behind all the difficult behaviour,
    I discovered a little, humble child, loved by God.
The experience of God's love,
    knowing that God is not disappointed in us
but is calling each one to grow in love ... today,
is a great mystery.

We tend to think that it is impossible for God to call us
    and to love us as we are today.
We feel we are not good enough,
that we are totally unworthy of that love.
Yet if we listen, God constantly reminds us:
    "I love you just as you are
    and I am calling you today, 'Come and be with me.'
    You may have been unfaithful at times
    because you forgot me;
    that is why I am leading you once more into the wilderness
    so that you can understand how much I love you
    and so that you may know me."

Let us take time to listen to God.
Perhaps we can just sit down near a tree,
like the girl who had written to me about her walk in the forest,
and hear God say to us:
    "You are beloved.
    You are precious in my eyes and I love you."

To become a friend of the weak and of those who are marginalised

To know God is to know the secrets of God.
To know Jesus is to know the secrets, the thirst of his heart.
St Gregory, in his commentary on the last words of Jesus
    on the cross, "I thirst",
tells us that "Jesus thirsts for us to thirst for him".
Jesus needs us to thirst for him
    so that he can communicate his love to us.

One of the greatest yearnings in the heart of Jesus
    is the yearning for unity.
Let us read over and over again the end of chapter 17 of John's
    Gospel
which are the final words of Jesus on community,
his final testimony on community life,
and in which he reveals the deep longing in his heart.

> "I do not pray for these only
> but also for those who believe in me through their word,
> that they may all be one;
> even as you, Father, are in me and I in you,
> that they may be in us,
> so that the world may believe that you have sent me.
> The glory which you have given me I have given to them,
> that they may be one even as we are one,
> I in them and you in me,
> that they may become perfectly one,
> so that the world may know that you have sent me
> and have loved them
> even as you have loved me.
> Father, I desire that they also, whom you have given to me,
> may be with me where I am,

to behold my glory which you have given me,
in your love for me
before the foundation of the world.
O righteous Father, the world has not known you,
but I have known you;
and these know that you have sent me.
I have made known to them your name,
and I will make it known,
that the love with which you have loved me
may be in them, and I in them." (vv. 20–6)

I am always touched to see how Jesus links unity and faith together:

"that they may all be one … so that the world may believe".

If Christians are united, this will help others to believe.
Disunity is an obstacle to faith
whether it be disunity between individuals, between groups
    or between churches.
Disunity prevents people from believing in the message of Jesus.
Our world is filled with divisions and disunity
and if we are not careful
    they seep into the life of our communities.
Whenever we allow barriers to rise up that isolate us
    FROM others then we can no longer connect.
Whenever we accept some people and reject others,
    we create barriers.
We need to ask the Holy Spirit to help us
    bring down these barriers,
otherwise we will remain closed up
    in the logic of fear and of exclusion
and become agents of disunity within our own community.
Jesus thirsts for unity and calls us all to unity.

Societies are generally built like pyramids,
    founded on a hierarchy of power:
at the top, there are a few rich and powerful people;

at the bottom a great number of weak and marginalised people;
in between there are different categories,
  more or less clearly identified.
At the very bottom –
  perhaps even outside the boundaries of the pyramid –
are all those who are rejected for one reason or another.
In India you will find the Tribal people at the bottom
  – some 50 million of them!
In the United States, the most recent immigrants
  are outside the boundaries of the pyramid.
In France or in Ireland, it is the travelling people, the gypsies,
  the "sans papiers"; those with no legal status.
In every society there are groups of people who are turned away
  by everybody.
Outside the pyramid you find people with mental disabilities
who are often considered "not fully human"
and who can thus be eliminated before birth
  or "put away" after birth.
Habits and attitudes of different societies may vary,
but you will find that every single culture
rejects and marginalises people with intellectual disabilities.
In certain African countries they are called "snake-children".
They should be given back to the snakes.
Thus they are abandoned in the bush, like Innocente,
whom we welcomed into l'Arche-Bouaké in the Ivory Coast.
In China, people with disabilities are often considered a
  punishment from God.
To take care of them is to go against the will of God.
In ancient cultures, amongst the Spartans, the Greeks and the
  Romans, children born with a handicap were killed:
  many are killed today.
How many times have I heard people say that it is a waste of time
  for us in l'Arche
to be with people "like that"!
How often people have looked at assistants in l'Arche
  with great admiration

implying that you have to be special, devoted,
in order to be with people "like that".

Other attitudes exist of course.
One day a friend of mine, who has a son with a very visible
handicap,
was sitting with him in a train station in France.
One of the porters who was from Kabylia in Algeria
came and asked: "Is he your son?"
When she answered "yes", he told her: "You are lucky.
In my village when a family has a child like yours,
we know that family is blessed by Allah."

A few years ago, I spoke to a group of parents of children in the
school run by l'Arche in Ouagadougou (Burkina Faso, West
Africa).
"Some people," I said, "may say that your children are crazy,
and many may despise them or be frightened of them
because of their disabilities.
But do you know that your child is a beloved child of God?
God welcomes in a special way those who are rejected by others.
In God's eyes they are a treasure."
An elderly Muslim man was there,
with a long beard and a beautiful face.
I had noticed him and the way he played
with his child who had a severe handicap.
This man raised his hand to speak and to thank me:
"No one has ever told us that our children are beloved of God,"
he said.
I could sense the weight of pain that had been lifted from this
man's heart.
I told him: "I see your face, the face of a wise man.
I sense a presence of God in you.
Many fathers need someone like you to help them better under-
stand their child."

People with disabilities can be a paradox.
Sometimes we are not quite sure who they are
    nor how to react to them.
Their presence obliges us to look more deeply into our own lives
and to reflect on what is really important.
We realise that our shared life with them in l'Arche is a treasure.
A secret has been entrusted to us.
People with disabilities are a sign, a presence of Jesus
    and a call to unity.
The weak and the poor are for us a source of unity.
Jesus came into the world to change and transform society
from a "pyramid"
    in which the strong and clever dominate at the top, into a "body",
    where each member of society has a place, is respected and is
    important.
In his first letter to the community in Corinth,
Paul speaks of the Church as a body,
    made up of different members.
Each one is important, not only because of their function
and the fact that each one is unique and irreplaceable
but also because when one member suffers, the whole body suffers.

> The eye cannot say to the hand, "I have no need of you"
> nor again the head to the feet, "I have no need of you."
> On the contrary, the parts of the body which seem weaker
> are necessary,
> and those parts of the body which we think less honourable,
> we invest with the greatest honour,
> and our unpresentable parts are treated with greater
> modesty —
> which our more presentable parts do not require.
> But God has so composed the body,
> giving the greater honour to the inferior part,
> that there may be no discord in the body,
> but that the members may have the same care for one
> another. (1 Cor 12:21–5)

It is the same for the body of humanity: each member is different,
    each is important,
yet there are parts of this body that we tend to hide.
Which members are they?
To whom was Paul referring?
I think he was referring in a particular way
    to people with disabilities
when he said that they are "necessary" and "should be honoured".
So often they are weak and hidden away.
If we are close to people who are weak and broken,
the pyramid will gradually be changed into a body
and we will live in unity, thanks to them.

Going down to meet Jesus

In his letter to the community in Philippi (Greece), Paul begins:

> So if there is any encouragement in Christ,
> any incentive of love, any participation in the Spirit,
> any affection and sympathy ... (Phil 2:1)

You can sense Paul's deep love for the Philippians.
They were the first people in Europe to whom he had brought the
    good news.
He was very attached to this community
    and in a special way to "Lydia"
who was one of the first to welcome him in Philippi.
The Philippians continually gave support to Paul
    throughout all his travels.
This had created a strong relationship
    between him and the community.
Paul calls them to unity, to remain united together:

> ... complete my joy by being of the same mind,
> having the same love,
> being in full accord and of one mind.

> Do nothing from selfishness or conceit,
> but in humility count others better than yourselves.
> Let each of you look not only to his own interests,
> but also to the interests of others. (Phil 2:2–4)

This is the cry, the yearning, of the heart of a father,
the founding father of the community,
who knows that unity brings life
and that disunity brings death.
Paul's heart, like the heart of Jesus, is filled with a love of unity,
   a desire for unity.

Then there are those amazing words of Paul which tell us clearly
how to become a source of unity:

> Have the same mind, the same sentiments that were in
> Christ Jesus ...

Paul describes or elaborates this "mind", these "sentiments":

> though he was in the form of God,
> he did not count equality with God
> a thing to be grasped,
> but he emptied himself, taking the form of a servant,
> being born in the likeness of men. (Phil 2:6–7)

Jesus did not try to preserve his status as God,
but allowed himself to be stripped, emptied,
and to become human
so that he could be seen, touched, heard,
become a human being like us,
a brother to us in humanity.

> And being found in human form he humbled himself
> and became obedient unto death,
> even death on a cross. (Phil 2:8)

Paul is describing God's way of being
which is not to be strong, wonderful and all powerful
but rather to be humble, to become human
    and to go down to the bottom
to become not only the servant but the rejected servant.
At the bottom of the social ladder
    he joins all those who have been rejected
and with them he creates a new order, a new community.
They are the starting point of this new creation,
    this new body of humanity
which has been torn apart – and continues to be torn apart
by the desire for power and prestige.

The vision of God is to go down the social ladder
    to take the lowest place
in order to *be with* the weak and the broken.
Then God rises up *with* them to build a new humanity
    which does not forget or exclude anyone.
Many people want to climb up the social ladder
of individual success and promotion,
to earn more, have more, to dominate,
to build up one's own personal glory and reputation.
The secret of Jesus is his simplicity and humility,
the way he embraces the lost and the broken,
and with them creates communities of hope,
    communities of the Kingdom.

This mystery was revealed in a particular way
when Jesus washed his disciples' feet (Jn 13).
He began by stripping himself of his outer garments
leaving only the garment of a servant.
Then he washed his disciples' feet, the gesture of a servant.
Peter was shocked;
he did not understand what Jesus was doing.
He cried out: "No! You shall never wash my feet!"
To which Jesus responded:

"If I do not wash you, you have no part in me"
which means: "If I do not wash your feet we are no longer friends.
You can leave.
Everything is over between us."
A very strong statement!
Peter was completely confused,
but he did not want to lose Jesus' friendship,
so he said: "Lord, not my feet only but also my hands and my head!"
Jesus replied: "No one who has bathed needs washing:
such a person is clean all over."
When he had finished washing the feet of the disciples
he said to them:

> "Do you understand what I have done to you?
> You call me Master and Lord and rightly; so I am.
> If I then, your Lord and Master, have washed your feet,
> you must wash each other's feet.
> I have given you an example."

He showed them the downward path of humility, service
and non-violence.

In another part of the gospel Jesus tells them:

> "When you give a lunch or a dinner,
> do not invite your friends or your brothers
> or your relations or rich neighbours ...
> No, when you have a banquet, invite the poor, the crippled,
> the lame and the blind and then you will be blessed."

(Lk 14:12–14)

In other words:
"Do not seek the company of the powerful and the influential
but go down the social ladder to meet the poor and the broken,
not to do things *for* them
but to *be with* them;

to enter into a heart to heart relationship with them,
to become their friend.
And if you become a friend of the weak
you will be blessed by God.
You will discover something entirely new.
You will discover that the gospel is truly 'good news'!"
It is a solution to the deep wounds of humanity,
a way to stop the cycle of violence and war,
the cycle of brotherly hatred as between Cain and Abel.
A cycle in which each one tries to push and hold down the other
motivated by the fear of being dominated by someone stronger.
Jesus tells us:

"Stop being so frightened and forever trying to protect
yourself!
Stop trying to defend and justify yourself!
Stop associating only with people like yourself!
Accept differences.
Go down the ladder.
Become a friend of the weak and the broken,
and a friend of God."

In our community in Bouaké (Ivory Coast)
we welcomed "Innocente",
a young girl who became a source of life
and great joy for the community.
She had been abandoned as a child, left to die in the bush.
She could have been bitten by a snake or killed by a wild animal
but somebody saw her there, picked her up
and took her to a local orphanage.
When she arrived at the orphanage she was like a skeleton;
she was dying.
Innocente survived all that,
and the orphanage later asked us to welcome her.
She was still quite small at the time
and we knew that she would never be able to walk or talk.
We could never quite understand what she was thinking,

but whenever anyone came near her and called her by name,
her whole face would light up.
She had an exceptional beauty.
She was completely incapable of judging or condemning anyone.
She was too fragile and weak to judge anyone.
But if people did not pay attention to her, she could feel hurt.
One day while I was looking at her, I thought to myself,
Jesus must be a bit like that:
neither judging nor condemning
but terribly wounded if we do not come close to him.

In our community one of my roles now
    is to accompany assistants
in their inner journey and in their community life.
When you spend the whole day listening to people,
    you learn a great deal,
much more than from books!
Books of course can be useful and interesting
but living words coming from a human heart are more alive,
precisely because they come from the heart, a living heart,
the place where God dwells,
the place also of our inner struggles.
One of the questions I often ask is: "Do you pray?"
I am not asking if they *say* prayers
but if they have "quiet times",
times of nourishment with the Word of God,
time alone to rest in God,
time to deepen their personal relationship with God.
The answer most of the time is "I do not have time",
and I can understand that.
There is so much to do in our daily lives in l'Arche
and as everywhere else we can become "too busy"!
In my own household, for example, many are growing older
    and need more medical care.
They can do less and less for themselves;
each one demands more presence and more time.

So I do understand that days are full.
But then I say something to assistants about their day off –
surely *then* they must have time for prayer?
This often leads to a moment of embarrassment
and if the person is truthful he usually admits
that he does not take time for prayer even then.
When I ask if it is because they don't *want* to pray,
the reply I often hear is, "I'm afraid to get too close to God
because he might ask something of me
    that I cannot or do not want to do."
As if God were there to oblige us
    to do things we do not want to do!
We have a strange notion of God.
It is linked, I think, to our fundamental sense of guilt,
a God who condemns and punishes,
a God who just wants to take away what we love,
a God who demands sacrifices.
But that is not God.
God is Love.
God is Mercy.
God loves each one of us and knows who we are.
God is never disappointed in us.
God knows our basic fears, our fear of not being loved ...
    even our fear of being loved.
God loves us just as we are
    and wants to reveal how deeply he respects us.

During one of our community weekends in northern France,
an assistant asked Frank, a man with disabilities, if he prayed.
He answered "Yes".
"What do you do when you pray, Frank?"
"I listen."
"What does God say to you?"
"God says to me, 'You are my beloved son,'" he replied.
That is what we discover in prayer:
    we are a beloved son, a beloved daughter, of God.

God wants to be united to us,
to reveal his presence to us
and to reveal to us
the mystery of Innocente, of Frank, of Luisito and of our own lives.
We are loved by God
as a "beloved" of God.

Our limits, wounds and handicaps may be less visible than theirs,
but they are just as real.
God's presence is also just as real
    within *our* weakness and *our* poverty too.

I came to a deeper understanding of this
    when I gave up my role of responsibility in the community
    and lived for a year as an assistant in "La Forestière",
one of our homes in Trosly for men and women with severe
    handicaps.
I was asked to take special care of Eric
which meant bathing him, helping him to eat
    and just spending time with him.
He taught me a great deal.
As I cared for his weak, little, wounded body,
    I began to understand more deeply
that he was the temple of God.
Paul's words to the Corinthians took on a deeper meaning for me:

> **"Do you not know that your body is the temple of the Holy
> Spirit?"** (1 Cor 6:19)

What an extraordinary gift it is to begin to understand
that our body is the place where God dwells,
    the place where God dwells amongst us!
That is true when we receive the consecrated bread and wine,
    body and blood of Jesus
at the eucharistic or communion services;
we are transformed into a tabernacle, a temple.

It is just as true when we love Jesus and long to keep his words.

> "Anyone who loves me will keep my word
> and my Father will love him
> and we shall come to him and make a home in him."
>
> (Jn 14:23)

Jesus reveals to us – as Paul does later –
and as the whole community of believers, the Church,
  continually reminds us throughout the ages:

> "Do you not know that you are the temple of God,
> that the Holy Spirit lives in you?" (1 Cor 3:16)

This little, fragile, wounded body of Eric is a temple of God!

We need quiet time, times of nourishment, alone with God
in order to enter more fully into this mystery of God's presence
  within us,
the mystery of our personal relationship with God.
I pray that my words will not be an obstacle but an instrument
that helps you to see and trust more fully in your own heart
and in the intuitions of your deepest self.
Perhaps that is all that Jesus wants to tell you today:
"Trust in yourself and in your own heart."
So I encourage you to take time alone in your room, in the forest,
  in a church or a chapel
just to be quiet and to listen to God.
God is leading and guiding each one of us,
helping us to become men and women of ever greater compassion
  and understanding.

DAY THREE

"If you but knew the gift of God"

(John 4:10)

Touching our wounds

As we take time alone with Jesus,
as we listen to his call,
we discover his love
but we also touch our pain and our sense of loss.
We tend to live in a world of illusion with regard to ourselves.
We so easily judge others
    but have trouble seeing ourselves as we really are.
Either we feel that we are extraordinary or else we feel that we are
    no good.
There is much inside of us that we do not want to look at.
People with alcohol problems for example rarely recognise or
    admit that they are addicted.
Jesus wants to teach us to know ourselves
    with our gifts, with our beauty,
with our deepest desire to love,
with our pain, our fragility, our vulnerability.

Let's look once again at the Samaritan woman
    and her encounter with Jesus.
She is one of the most wounded people in the whole gospel.
She belongs to a rejected race
and her own people seem to have cast her aside.
I often wondered why she came to fetch water "at noon".
In countries like hers, women usually go to collect water early in
    the morning
when the sun is not yet too hot.
They usually go at about the same time
so that they can all meet and talk around the well,
share about their lives,
    their difficulties, their children, their husbands.
If a woman of ill repute arrives, tension can arise.

Others make remarks or make fun of her or move away from her.
She does not feel comfortable;
she does not feel she belongs to this little community of village
    women;
she does not share their way of life nor the same concerns.
She scandalises them.
I think that is why the Samaritan woman comes at noon,
    even though the sun is at its zenith.
But maybe I am mistaken.
When I meet her in heaven I will ask her if what I said about her
    was true.
I won't be a bit surprised if she tells me that I completely missed
    the point,
and that she had come at that late hour simply because she had
    overslept!!
It is clear, however, that her situation made it difficult for her
to meet others in public places as well as in places of worship.
She was a broken woman,
rejected by the sanctimonious people around her;
she must have thought that God too had rejected her.
Maybe she was from a broken background
    that had only known misery:
no family, no home, no stable love, no security,
a situation that filled her with sadness and anger and locked her in
    guilt and revolt.
Maybe she felt sad and angry with herself, with her children,
    and with the people around her.

John's Gospel tells us that Jesus is tired
and so sits down near the well of Jacob in Samaria.
It is moving to sense Jesus' exhaustion, his humanity.
He is so "like us in all things except sin".
We need to pay close attention to Jesus in his humanity,
be close to him in his tiredness.
He can show us how to live our tiredness and our humanity.

The woman arrives with a jug on her head or shoulder to fetch
    water.
Jesus turns to her and asks: **"Give me to drink".**
He does not begin by telling this woman to get her act together
but rather by expressing his need and asking if she can help him.

The fact that this encounter takes place at a well is significant.
Scripture tells us about three other important encounters
    that took place near a well
and that were sealed in a deep covenant.
The first involved Abraham's servant who was sent to find a wife
    for Abraham's son.
When the servant reaches the well he meets Rebecca and says:

      "Give me something to drink." (cf. Gen 24)

The second concerned the meeting between Jacob and Rachel (cf.
    Gen 29).
The third was Moses and Zipporah (cf. Ex 2).
At the well in Samaria,
    Jesus himself meets this broken, rejected woman
and reveals to her her value, her importance;
reveals that she can become a source of life and be fruitful.

This Samaritan woman truly existed
    and Jesus really spoke to her.
One day, in heaven, we too will be able to meet and speak to her!
We must be careful of interpretations of the gospel
    which are only symbolic.
They can be interesting but it is important to look at the facts,
    at the concrete reality,
and see what they tell us.
The Samaritan woman is both a reality and a symbol
(like others in Scripture),
    because she teaches us something about humanity
      and about our own selves.

She tells us something important about those who are weak,
     broken, excluded, marginalised;
all those we usually do not want to see
     or that we pretend do not exist,
those we put away in institutions and prisons
     out of sight of the rest of society;
those who are hidden in slum areas.

This woman also lives within each one of us;
she is the wounded, broken part of our being
     that we hide from others,
and even from our own selves.
She symbolises the place of guilt in us
from which are born many of our attitudes and actions –
consciously or unconsciously.
This sense of guilt can even urge us to be heroic and generous
in order to redeem ourselves.
It can also push us into anger
     and dependence on drugs and alcohol.
If we do not let God penetrate
     into the shadow areas of our being,
they risk governing our lives.

I remember talking about the Samaritan to a group
in which there was a woman with a serious alcohol problem.
She used to go through times of abstinence
but then would fall back into drinking.
She would stop again and again and then start drinking.
After my talk she came up to me and said:
"Now I understand. There are two women living inside me.
The one who drinks
and the one who, when she is not drinking,
refuses to look at the wounded part of me,
as if it was too dirty for God to love.
I deny that that part exists
     and I only speak to God about the bright side of me.

I understand now that I have to let God meet
  the wounded, broken woman inside of me
and let him enter into all the dirt inside me."
Without realising it and in her own rough language
  she was uttering the words of John in the prologue to his gospel:
  "the light came into the darkness".

If we deny the existence of darkness within ourselves
because we think we are pure,
  then the light cannot come into us.
So too, if we think we are only darkness, unworthy of God,
we close up in our darkness;
  we cut ourselves off from the light
and prevent it from entering into our lives.

This is precisely the mystery of the Incarnation:
God wants to enter into our very being.
God knows how wounded we are.
God knew how broken the woman from Samaria was,
the hurt she had lived with, perhaps from birth;
just as God knows the wounds of our early childhood.
God is aware of the world of darkness, fear and guilt
  that develops in our lives
even before we become aware of it.
God yearns to enter precisely into that part of our being
that is obscure, broken and in pain
in order to liberate us.

This Samaritan woman lives in me and in you,
in all those parts of our being where we feel guilty
  of not loving others as we should.
Men often do not know how to love and care for their wives,
or women for their husbands, and they feel guilty.
Parents often feel they do not love their children enough,
or children their parents.
We are all caught up in the same inability to love.

When Jesus speaks to this woman, he is speaking to you and to me.

Jesus sits down by the well, in a position below the woman,
    more humble than the woman.
He has to look up at her – he has to look up at her in me;
then he shows me his need, **"Give me something to drink."**
Our reaction is generally like hers:
"How can you, Jesus, ask me for something!
How can you come to one who feels so weak and broken!
I'm too insignificant, too unworthy,
    for you to ask something of me."

This is our spontaneous reaction
just like Peter's reaction at the washing of the feet:
"It is not possible that you put yourself lower than me!"
Then Jesus says to the Samaritan woman:
    "If you but knew the gift of God ... "
If we only knew the gift of God ...

In order for us to listen to God saying "Give me to drink";
in order for us not to run away from him;
in order for us to accept and be open
    to our wounds as well as to our gifts;
– we need time and we need silence.

To discover the source of living water

This encounter between Jesus and the Samaritan woman
    announces a covenant.
It is a moment of communion, of tenderness and of truth.
Jesus is going to reveal to her
    that she will find the waters to quell her thirst,
not only in Jacob's well
but within her inner "well", her own heart, her deepest self.

    "If you but knew the gift of God

and who it is that is saying to you, 'Give me to drink',
rather you would have asked him
and he could have given you living water." (Jn 4:10)

She is surprised by his words and does not understand:

"Lord," she says, "you have no bucket to draw from the well
and the well is deep.
Where will you find the living water?
Are you greater than our Father Jacob, who gave us this well,
drank from it himself and gave water to his family and all the
animals?" (vv. 11–12)

Jesus replies:

"Whoever drinks of the waters that I will give,
will never be thirsty."

Then he adds some of the most extraordinary words in the whole
gospel:

"The waters that I will give will become [in that person] a
spring of water
welling up in eternal life." (v. 14)

This extraordinary promise was made to this wounded, broken
   woman of Samaria;
this woman full of guilt.
Jesus tells her that she will become a spring of water for others.
She will give them new life, the very life of God,
for water is a symbol of life.
He is telling her: "You will bear much fruit."

Jesus yearns for us to become fully alive
and so to communicate life to others.
The giving of life is one of the most amazing mysteries of creation.

Spiders give birth to spiders
    who in turn give birth to other spiders and so on.
Giraffes give birth to giraffes, apples to apples:
there is an infinite, uninterrupted flow of life.

There are of course different ways of giving life.
There is first of all the biological transmission of life:
a man and woman unite and give birth to a child.
That physical birth is only the beginning.
In order for a child to grow and develop
    and to communicate life in turn to others,
he/she needs security, love and tenderness.
A child needs to live in a stable relationship of love,
a bonding with his mother, his father and others around him/her.
We human beings are made for love,
called to live covenant relationships
within which we give life to one another.

It does not really matter if a mother spider does not love her baby
    spiders!
But if a child has not known a special, unique love
the life of the child is in danger.
This love is not an ideal but a real struggle day after day.
We are all struggling to grow in love.
No parent, no person, is perfect.
But each one of us, with our personal stories,
is called to growth in love.

When I was thirteen I lived a very strong experience
    which was like a new birth for me
— my third "birth" ... the first one being my birth day, the second
    my baptism ...
I wanted to enter the Royal Naval School in England.
War was already raging and we were living in Canada.
I would have to cross the Atlantic
at a time when one out of every five boats

was being sunk by German submarines.
I went to see my father and told him what I wanted to do.
He asked me why.
I am not sure what I answered
      but I will never forget what he said to me:
"I trust you.
If that is what you want, you have to do it."

That day, with those words, my father gave me new life
I experienced a sort of rebirth.
If my father had confidence in me
that meant I could have confidence in myself.

If he had told me to wait until I was older
      and had more experience
I probably would have waited
but I would have lost confidence in my own intuitions.
His reply: "I trust you" not only gave me confidence in myself
but it has helped me throughout my life to trust others.

When we love someone, we give life to that person.
When we love, we trust
and reveal to people their value, their beauty,
and their capacity to give life to others.
When Jesus told this woman that she would become a
"spring of water welling up in eternal life"
he was revealing to her the deep hidden source of life in her.
We do not always recognise this spring of life within us.
We know that we have a certain intelligence
and are aware of our emotions, desires and compulsions,
but we are often unaware of the deep well, the sanctuary of love,
      within us
and our capacity to love with the very love of God.
We may in fact be frightened of this loving tenderness
      that we sense rising within us
because we see it as a weakness

or as something linked only to our sexuality.
This can fill us with confusion.

Yet within this very gentleness and tenderness of our hearts,
there is a presence of God.
We often experience this most strongly
when we are with people with profound disabilities.
The mystery Jesus revealed to the Samaritan woman
is the mystery contained in the life of each one of us:
if we drink from the source of life, which is Jesus,
we too will become a source of life;
we will bring life, the very life of God, into our world.
Thus we fulfil the deepest desire of Jesus for us:
his desire that we become men and women who are fully alive.

To welcome the person within us
who is weak and poor

The Samaritan woman was confused; she did not understand.
She says to Jesus:
   "Lord, give me these waters that I may not thirst" (Jn 4:15).
Jesus changes the conversation:
"Go and call your husband and come back" (v. 16).

Jesus is so gentle and understanding.
He does not judge or condemn this woman.
He simply wants to draw her attention to her wounds, her fragility
and to show her the place of pain and sadness
that she has been hiding from others and even from herself.

"I have no husband," she replies.
"You are right in saying, 'I have no husband'," says Jesus,
"for you have had five husbands
and the man you have now is not your husband.
What you have said is true" (vv. 17–18).
That little phrase "What you have said is true" is important.

Jesus wants to help her to discover the truth of her being,
to realise who she is, with all her brokenness;
to show in this way that he does not judge her or condemn her.
The only thing that matters is that we be truthful;
that we do not let ourselves be governed by lies and by illusion.
Once she has accepted the truth of her being, she can become a
    spring of life.
It is only when we have accepted the truth of our being
that we, like the Samaritan woman, can begin to walk
    the path of inner wholeness.

We need to touch the truth of who we are.
It is then, as we grow gradually into the acceptance of our wounds
    and fragility,
that we grow into wholeness,
and from that wholeness, life begins to flow forth
    to others around us.

It is important to take time to be silent, to be alone with Jesus,
to look at the reality of who we are,
be in contact with our hidden places of pain
and little by little we can become a friend of our weakness.

In 1980, when I left the role of community leader in Trosly,
I lived a year at "La Forestière", one of our homes
for ten men and women with profound disabilities.
I have told you about Eric but there was also Lucien.
Lucien was born with severe mental and physical disabilities.
He cannot talk or walk or move his arms.
His body is a bit twisted
    and he has to remain in his wheelchair or in his bed.
He never looks anyone directly in the eyes.
Lucien's father died when he was twelve.
He lived the first thirty years of his life with his mother
who cared for him and understood him and his needs;
she could interpret all his body language.

He was at peace and felt secure with her.
One day she fell sick and had to go to the hospital.
Lucien was put into another hospital
and was plunged into a totally strange and unknown world;
he had lost all his familiar points of reference;
no one seemed to understand him.
Screams of anguish rose up in him
    which were unbearable to hear.
Finally he came to "La Forestière".
When faced with his constant screaming we felt quite powerless.
If we tried to touch him to calm him down,
this very touch seemed to increase his anguish.
There was nothing to do but to wait.

The pitch of Lucien's scream was piercing
and seemed to penetrate the very core of my being,
awakening my own inner anguish.
I could sense anger, violence and even hatred rising up within me.
I would have been capable of hurting him to keep him quiet.
It was as if a part of my being that I had learned to control
    was exploding.
It was not only Lucien's anguish
    that was difficult for me to accept
but the revelation of what was inside my own heart,
— my capacity to hurt others —
I who had been called to share my life with the weak,
had a power of hatred for a weak person!

That experience, and other similar experiences, helped me towards
    a better understanding of the mothers of "battered children";
women who have been abandoned by their husbands
    or partners;
an abandonment which gives rise to loneliness,
    anguish and depression within them.
They usually have to work for a living
    and are bringing up their children alone.

When they come home from a full day's work, they are tired;
they have just enough energy to make dinner
     and to put the children in front of the television!
But children of course need more than that.
They are yearning for love and attention and presence.
So they start crying, even screaming.
The mother is exhausted; her inner "well" is empty.
Their cry for attention and love reveals her own need for love.
There is so much anguish and inner pain in her
that she ends up by hitting one of the children
in order to make him be quiet
— and especially to liberate her own anguish!

How painful it is for us to look reality in the face,
to discover our own fragility
     and our capacity for anger and hatred.
The temptation is so great to avoid or run away from
those who reveal our inner limits and brokenness.
The roots of much racism, rejection and exclusion are here.
It is important not to run away,
but to find someone with whom we can speak about these shadow
     areas of our being,
these inner "demons", the "wolf" within us,
someone who can help us not to be controlled by them
so that they no longer haunt our lives.

When I was living in the Forestière, I was given a text by Carl
     Jung, the analytical psychologist and disciple of Freud.
It was a letter he had written to a young Christian woman which
     I quote from memory.
He said something like this, referring to the words of Jesus in
     Matthew 25:

     I admire Christians,
     because when you see someone who is hungry or thirsty,
     you see Jesus.

When you welcome a stranger, someone who is "strange",
you welcome Jesus.
When you clothe someone who is naked, you clothe Jesus.
What I do not understand, however,
is that Christians never seem to recognise Jesus
in their own poverty.
You always want to do good to the poor outside you
and at the same time you deny the poor person
living inside you.
Why can't you see Jesus in your own poverty,
in your own hunger and thirst?
In all that is "strange" inside you:
in the violence and the anguish that are beyond your control!
You are called to welcome all this, not *to deny* its existence,
but to accept that it is there and to meet Jesus there.

Jung's letter helped me to realise
that I cannot welcome and receive Jesus
unless I welcome my own weakness, my poverty
and my deepest needs.
I cannot accept the wounds of Innocente, Eric and Lucien
unless I am open and accept my own wounded self and seek help.
Can I truly be compassionate towards them
if I am not compassionate towards myself?

The mystery of the weak and the broken is that they call forth
not only the deep well of love and tenderness in us
but also the hardness and darkness.
Jesus calls us not only to welcome the weak and the rejected,
like Claudia and Lucien,
but also the weak and the broken person within us
and to discover the presence of Jesus within us.

That is the meaning of the words of Jesus
to the woman from Samaria:
"What you have said is true."

In order for us to be men and women who give life to others
we have to live in the truth of who we are;
we have to find an inner wholeness,
no longer to deny or ignore our wounds
    but to welcome them
and to discover the presence of God
    in these very places of our own weakness.

DAY FOUR

"Love one another as I have loved you"

(John 15:12)

Learning to live together

Our life with Jesus begins with an invitation: "Come"
or "Today I want to come to your home"
or a call to mission: "Go, sell all and follow me."

Everything begins with a personal, heart to heart
    encounter with Jesus.
Then Jesus helps us to meet others who have had a similar call.
Each one is different but each has received an invitation from Jesus.
He calls us together; we build community.

I love to read over and over again the different gospel stories
which show our common humanity.
As soon as Jesus is absent, for example,
    his disciples start comparing
to see who is the best, the greatest, the most competent!
Then, some of the mothers intervene for their sons ...
    as one might expect!
Imagine the mother of James and John coming up to Jesus
and asking him if her two sons could have the first and the best
    places in the Kingdom!
Imagine the reaction of Peter, Matthew and the others!

The gospel is so profoundly human.
Jesus knows our hearts
and the deep roots of rivalry and jealousy within us.
Each of us has such a deep yearning to be loved or admired.
It is not easy for us to share our lives with others
    in family or in community.
As soon as people come and live together
they seek the best place,
and to be seen as important.

They seek to show that they are stronger than others;
   that they know better than others.

But Jesus calls us to share our lives together.
We will experience conflict
and hopefully we shall realise that we are not in fact as loving as
   we thought!
We are drawn to some people; others we dislike.
What do we do when we discover this?
Some of us close up in depression,
others escape into denial or addiction;
sometimes we are eaten up with jealousy
  or overwhelmed by hatred and anger, accusing others.

It is important that we experience the reality of our limited love;
the reality of our broken hearts.
Only then can we begin to understand
   what Jesus was asking his disciples when he said:
   "Love one another."
We may react quite quickly … "No, I can't love *that* person!"
And Jesus replies:

> **"But I tell you who are listening:**
> **Love your enemies, do good to those who hate you,**
> **bless those who curse you,**
> **pray for those who treat you badly."** (Lk 6:27–8)

It is easy, he tells us, to love those who love us,
who shower us with compliments.
But Jesus is asking us to love our "enemies".

Our enemy is not necessarily some foreigner
but could be someone quite close
   in our own family or community; someone at work.
The "enemy" is someone who seems to threaten us
and prevents us from being ourselves;

someone who blocks our freedom and creativity
and who provokes depression or aggression in us
   by their very presence.

When we have some quiet time,
it is important to ask God to show us who is our enemy.
It is perfectly natural for us to have people who have hurt us
and awaken our defence mechanisms –
that is a part of who we are,
part of our common humanity.

A woman came up to me after a talk I gave
and told me that she had discovered that her husband
   was her enemy:
"He is happy when I do all the cooking and the housework,
but he never really listens to me
   or asks my opinion about anything.
He treats me as if I did not exist.
I have so much anger in me against him."

During a retreat, a man told me that he could not understand why
he had so many problems with his eldest son.
He said: "Every time he opens his mouth, he exasperates me.
No matter what he says, I contradict him
   and I just want him to be quiet.
It is not like that with the two other children.
I can listen to them."
He did not see why he reacted like that.
A few days later he came back to see me and said:
"I'm beginning to understand my rejection of my eldest son.
He reminds me of my own faults.
When I reject him I am actually rejecting everything in me
   that I cannot accept."
This man was discovering that his eldest son
   was not actually his "enemy"
but that he was, himself, his own enemy!

When we become more aware of who our enemy is,
then we can hear the words of Jesus: "Love him. Love her!"
We become conscious of all the resistances in us.
"No, I can't do it! That person has hurt me too much!
You are asking too much of me. It is impossible!"
And Jesus may reply: "Yes, you're right. You cannot do it.
But do you want me to help you?
Do you trust me?
Do you trust that 'nothing is impossible for God'?"

In order to be true followers of Jesus
we have to discover this trust that "nothing is impossible for God".
We need Jesus and his Holy Spirit to do what we are called to do;
we cannot do it all by ourselves.

In the gospel story Mark tells us about a rich young man
   who approached Jesus.
Jesus told him to "go and sell" what he had,
and to give this money to the poor
and then follow him (Mk 10:21).
The young man was terribly sad and walked away
because he had "great wealth",
which he was not prepared to let go.
Jesus too must have been sad.
Later he said to his disciples:

> "How hard it is for those who have riches to enter the
> kingdom of God!"
> The disciples were astounded by these words, but Jesus
> insisted. "My children," he said to them, "how hard it is to
> enter the kingdom of God. It is easier for a camel to pass
> through the eye of a needle than for someone rich to enter
> the kingdom of God."
> They were more astonished than ever, saying to one another,
> "In that case who can be saved?"
> Jesus looked at them steadily and said,

**"Humanly speaking it is impossible, but not for God
because for God everything is possible." (Mk 10:24–7)**

We are not truly disciples of Jesus until we have discovered that
"for God everything is possible";
that which is impossible for us, is possible for God.

This means that disciples of Jesus must learn
how to face difficulties and impossible situations;
not to run away from them,
but to discover that God will give us the necessary strength
because **"nothing is impossible to God"**.
As long as we see our life in community and our desire to serve
 others
as something *we have* chosen, we are not yet living the covenant.
If we think that it depends only on us;
that our bonding to others in family or in community
is the fruit of our own efforts, we are not yet living the covenant.
Covenant is a gift of God.
We need a new strength from God
 to live covenant relationships day after day.
Our covenant with God, in l'Arche, is revealed when we can say,
"I can't do it! I can't continually live my life with these people!
But I know that God can help me to do it."
It's as if we have to touch our own limitations and weakness
when faced with the needs of the poor and the weak
before we can discover that only God
 can change our hearts and our lives.

We cannot live and grow in peace with others
until we discover that forgiveness is at the heart
 of the gospel message.
God's response to conflict and division is reconciliation.
Reconciliation is a gift of God
 that allows us not to be governed by feelings of guilt;
feelings which can paralyse us, make us depressed or aggressive

[73]

and fill us with self-doubt.
Through his forgiveness Jesus liberates us from guilt
and makes us men and women, truly alive and truly free.

To forgive is first of all
    to recognise the covenant that bonds us together in love.
It is not just a question of hugging or embracing someone
    to show we forgive them.
It is the recognition that there is a bonding given by God
    which is deeper than our feelings;
that our "enemy" too has a place
    in the community, the family, the church or society;
the "enemy" has a right to live and to flourish.
Jesus has called the "enemy" to a specific place
    and has given him or her specific gifts
which I should respect.
Forgiveness is a long process
that begins with this respect for the other; for the "enemy".

A young man told me after a retreat:
    "I thought about the covenant with my own father.
    I had been hurt by him when I was young.
    He was so authoritarian; he never listened to me
    and seemed to enjoy putting me down.
    I left home because I couldn't stand it any more.
    During this week, I became aware not only of the covenant
    with those in community
    but also of the covenant with my father.
    I am starting to understand him and to forgive him."

I suggested that he go and see his father,
    but he immediately replied:
        "No. I'm not ready yet. I'm still too vulnerable.
    I still feel quite fragile.
    If I go to see him now he will crush me. I need more time."
His reaction was wise.

We are like twisted, knotted trees that need to be straightened
if they are to grow and to give new life.
This young man was beginning to accept his father,
to see the covenant that existed between himself and his father,
but he needed time
    and a renewed sense of the presence of the Holy Spirit
before he could meet his father face to face.

Not long ago I was told the story of a woman
who had been put in gaol through a man's false testimony.
During her time in prison, this woman had a real,
    personal encounter with God.
She told the religious sister who had helped her
that she could not forgive the man who had made her suffer so
    much,
"but," she added, "I pray each day that God will forgive him".
She too had started on the road to forgiveness.
In the depths of her heart she had forgiven this man,
but this forgiveness had not yet permeated her being.
Her feelings had not changed.
She needed time.
The man also needed time to discover the evil in him.

Forgiveness is a gift of God.
Forgiveness is the heart of the gospel message;
the heart of the family and the heart of community life.
Forgiveness begins with the recognition
    that we are bonded together
in community and in a common humanity.
God has created each one of us,
    each one is precious and important.
In order to be faithful to our covenant
    in l'Arche, in our family or in society
we need to become men and women of forgiveness.

To stay with Jesus

Jesus spoke a lot about forgiveness.
He healed and liberated the hearts
  of many wounded and broken people,
who had been crushed and pushed down
by the weight of stringent laws.
He himself was wounded by the pettiness and jealousy
of certain scribes and Pharisees who were trying to trap him
  (cf. Jn 8:2–11).

One day, they bring to Jesus a woman
who has been caught committing adultery.
They have not brought her
  because they are concerned about her well-being,
or interested in her as a person
but because they want to use her and to use her situation
  in order to embarrass Jesus and to trap him.
According to the law of Moses, such a woman should be stoned.
If Jesus speaks of forgiveness,
they will say he is contradicting the law of Moses.
If he speaks of conforming to this law,
  then he is contradicting himself
and all that he has been saying about mercy and forgiveness.
Jesus is silent.
He bends down and starts writing on the ground with his finger.
No one knows what he wrote, but he is there, writing silently.

The scribes persist in anger:

  "And you, what do you say?"

Jesus stands up, looks at them and says:

  **"Let the one among you who is without sin
  be the first to throw the stone at her."**

[76]

Bending down again he continues to write on the ground.
The gospel tells us that the men began to leave one by one,
starting with the eldest who, according to the law,
   should throw the first stone.
They all left.
Jesus remained there, standing alone with the woman.
We can easily imagine the fear, the shame, the anguish in her,
faced with the horror of being stoned to death!
It is probably the first time she has ever seen this man from
   Nazareth
who has just liberated her.

The tone of Jesus' voice seems to change as he addresses her:
"Woman, where are they? Has no one condemned you?"
"No one, Sir," she replies.
"Neither do I condemn you," says Jesus,
"go and sin no more."
Jesus did not come to condemn her – nor us!
Jesus comes to give her life – to give us life.

This gospel passage can be difficult for some of us to accept
   or to understand.
In the fourth century, people in the Church questioned its
   authenticity.
Some versions of the Bible have left it out completely.
It seems too ambiguous.
Jesus *surely must have* condemned adultery!

In the writings of the prophets such as Ezekiel,
   adultery was a symbol of sin;
of our turning away from God, the divine Creator and Lover;
of being unfaithful to the One who loves, protects
   and nourishes us;
a symbol of "drinking" from sources other than the Source of Life.

To understand this passage we have to understand what sin is.

Sin is not merely a question of transgressing some moral or
    religious law.
It is much more.
Throughout Holy Scripture,
    and particularly in the gospels and in Paul's letters,
sin is depicted as "turning one's back on God",
"losing trust in Jesus",
"no longer believing in his words and promises",
"doubting the existence of the covenant".
We are then no longer nourished by God's presence
in the Word of God
in the Eucharist
in prayer
in the poor.
To sin is to cut ourselves off from Jesus.
When we are cut off,
    we will surely transgress rules and regulations;
for we will not have the strength to obey any laws
    or fulfil any obligations.

In order to live the "good news",
to love our enemies,
to be close to the weak and the forgotten,
to be faithful to the covenant given in community or in marriage,
to live a life of love day after day,
we need to be connected to the Source of Life,
to be in communion with the One who *is* Life, Jesus.

When Jesus says, **"Go and sin no more"**,
he is actually saying, "Go and remain in my love.
    Stay with me.
    Choose life.
    Find nourishment in my love and in my presence.
    Choose what gives you life, what is good for you."

We have to be careful because some food can be poisonous.

Certain films, relationships, places or ways of living
may also be like poison for us.
They can gradually turn us away from Jesus
and can even hurt us
and the good news that we are called to live.
If we are dead inside,
we will not give life to others but only death.
If we want to be fully alive, so that we can give life
we have to discern what is good nourishment for each one of us,
and choose "good food".
We need Jesus,
  in the Word
  in the Eucharist
  in prayer
and in his mysterious presence in the weak and the poor,
so that we can be fully alive.

To forgive and to be forgiven

To forgive is to rediscover the bonds that bind us together.
We are no longer separate from each other;
we are one in God.

Mark the evangelist tells us about another incident
when Jesus was preaching in a house in Capernaum.
A crowd of people filled the house;
no one could get through the door!
In order to reach Jesus, four men made an opening in the roof
and lowered a stretcher on which a paralytic man lay.
Jesus was preaching.
Suddenly the man was in front of him.
This man was paralysed; he could neither speak nor walk,
he just looked intensely at Jesus.

People who are paralysed and unable to speak often "say" so much
just through the look in their eyes; they "speak" with their eyes.

When this man was in front of Jesus his eyes must have said:
"I love you. I trust you. Have mercy on me."
Jesus was touched by his faith
and he said to the paralysed man:
    "My child, your sins are forgiven" ...
which means "You are free!"
In the crowd of course there was some grumbling.
Some scribes were shocked, surprised and even angered.
How could he talk like that!
They had never heard such words
or read such things in their theology books.
This man was blaspheming!
How could he forgive sin!
Only God can forgive sin!
Jesus, aware of what they were thinking, looked at them and said:

> "Why do you have such thoughts in your hearts?
> Which of these is easier: to say to the paralysed man,
> 'Your sins are forgiven'
> or to say, 'Get up, pick up your stretcher and walk'?
> But to prove to you that the Son of Man has authority
> to forgive sins on earth"
> – he said to the paralysed man –
> "I order you: get up, pick up your stretcher
> and go off home." (Mk 2:8–11)

And of course the man jumped up!

It is a very powerful scene.
Imagine the eyes of this man who loves Jesus,
the anger and concern of the scribes and Pharisees
and the loving, provocative gesture of Jesus –
the mystery of his forgiveness.
When he tells the man to "get up and walk",
he is in fact saying the same thing as "your sins are forgiven".
He is lifting from his shoulders the weight that was crushing him.

He is liberating him from the heaviness of guilt
that was suffocating him,
hindering his growth in love.
He is assuring this man of God's love for him;
that he is no longer separated from God
but in communion with God.
It is as if this man suddenly received wings to fly!

Jesus lives in the eternal present moment.
At every moment of our day he loves us
and assures us of his love.
We, however, often close ourselves up
– out of fear, or in remorse and disgust at ourselves.
That is why we need forgiveness
which reopens the doors of our hearts
and reminds us over and over again:
    "You are my beloved son;
    you are my beloved daughter.
    I am not interested in the past
    and not worried about the future.
    I am with you *today*.
    I want to live with you and in you
    so that together we can give life to others."
Forgiveness brings us back to our first love,
our first experience of the love of God and of his promise:

      "I will betroth you forever
      and you will know God." (Hos 2)

Jesus knows the weight of our guilt.
He knows our need to be forgiven
and to hear words of forgiveness.
In his great tenderness,
he chooses some of us – who are no better than others –
human like us in their fragility.
He chooses some to whom he gives the ministry of forgiveness;

to whom he says,
"You will forgive sins in my name.
You will represent me in the sacrament of forgiveness."
It is important to be able to share with someone
who knows how to listen with understanding and compassion
to all that has hurt us;
all that we have failed to do,
all that we regret,
all that fills our hearts, preventing us from living in hope.

When we can put words on the inner darkness we are living
it is a liberating experience.
The more wounded we are, the more we tend to wound others.
The more anguished and guilty we feel,
the more we doubt God's love,
and then the more we turn away from God.
We need to talk to someone who listens, understands and has
mercy on us.
To forgive and to be forgiven;
to liberate and to be liberated
isn't that the goal of our lives?
To be a presence of the forgiving, compassionate God:
Forgive us our trespasses
as we forgive those who have trespassed against us (Matt 6:12)

DAY FIVE

*"O God, my God, why have you
forsaken me?"*

(Mark 15:34)

Entering into pain

Jesus came into the world to re-create it,
to give it back its full meaning
to take away our limited vision of life,
a vision which prevents the birth of hope
and which paralyses us in front of all that seems impossible.
Yet **"nothing is impossible for God"**.

If we do not take time to enter more deeply
   into the heart of silence
so that we can participate in this new creation;
if we do not allow the grace of Jesus to fill us more completely,
we risk becoming "burnt out".
It is impossible to live all that has to be done in our communities
if we lose our sense of what is unique to l'Arche.
Many of us have been taught, for example,
that we should "*do good to*" the poor.
The gospel message tells us that it is the *poor who* **do good to us**.
A mother knows full well that her little child gives her life
just by the way he looks at her, smiles at her,
calls her, loves her and needs her.

Human beings grow from the dependence of a child
to the independence of an adult.
In our journey with Jesus it is just the opposite:
we adults are called to become more and more
   like little children.
It is a reversal of our attitudes and certitudes.
We do not enter the Kingdom of God by becoming
more knowledgeable, more influential, more powerful;
but by becoming more humble, more gentle, more loving.
The Kingdom of God is the communion of hearts.

If we enter into personal relationships
with those who are weak and lonely,
— not just to *do good to them* but to *be with* them
then we enter into a personal relationship with God.
And as we begin to celebrate life together
so we discover the heart of God.

Many of us were taught "an eye for an eye, a tooth for a tooth".
This is the general rule in many of our societies.
It is normal to want to protect oneself
and to respond to aggression with aggression or repression.
Yet Jesus tells us,
> **"Love your enemies.**
> **Do good to those who hate you** [Matt 5:44].
> Let go of your defence mechanisms.
> You do not need to protect yourselves
> for *I* am your protection."

Hope for our world lies not in the manufacture of greater weapons
or the implementation of more repressive laws;
hope lies in our capacity to love and to forgive
and in our desire to live reconciliation
   and to grow in love for our enemies.

Our spontaneous reaction to suffering is repulsion.
We are frightened of pain:
the most common response to the existence of pain
is to be scandalised by it and to seek to eliminate it.
Some philosophers justify the existence of pain;
some stoics and spiritual masters teach us
how to remain serene in the face of pain
through an attitude of detachment and through will power;
but Jesus brings a whole new meaning to pain.

Jesus did not die serenely but in agony.
In the Garden of Olives he was frightened and

his sweat fell to the ground like great drops of blood.

(Lk 22:44)

He begged the Father,

"May this cup be taken away from me ..." (Lk 22:42)

On the cross he cried out:

"My God, my God, why have you forsaken me?" (Mk 15:34)

It is important to enter into the mystery of pain,
the pain of our brothers and sisters in countries that are at war,
the pain of our brothers and sisters who are sick,
   who are hungry, who are in prison;
brothers and sisters who do not know where they will sleep
   this night;
it is important to enter into the pain of all those
   for whom no one cares
and who are alone;
all those who are living grief and loss.

To help us enter into this mystery of pain and to realise our fear of it,
let us look at a passage in Matthew's Gospel.

Jesus has just confirmed Peter as "the rock", the "foundation stone"
on which the Church will be built.
Jesus puts order into the group
– organisation and order are important in a group.
Then, almost immediately afterwards, he starts to tell them of his
   departure:

> **From then onwards Jesus began to make it clear to his disciples
> that he was destined to go to Jerusalem and suffer grievously
> at the hands of the elders and chief priests and scribes
> and to be put to death
> and to be raised upon the third day. (16:21)**

Jesus does not say directly that he will be leaving,
but he tells them that he is going to suffer a great deal
     and be put to death.
You can imagine the desperation of these men who love him
and who have left everything to follow him,
who have perhaps been criticised by their family and their friends
for their trust in him.

Something collapses inside them.
They cannot bear the thought that Jesus will suffer and die;
their hopes are shattered.
Peter's reaction was generous and kind.
He took Jesus aside and rebuked him saying,

>   **"No! That will not happen"**

as if he wanted to reassure Jesus – and reassure himself –
he wanted to help Jesus to get rid of his gloomy thoughts.
Jesus' reaction to Peter was strong, full of sadness
     and perhaps full of anger:

>   **"Get behind me, Satan!"** (Satan in Hebrew means "adversary")
>   **"You are an obstacle for me"**

which can also be translated as "You are a scandal to me".
There is a play on words here
as the Greek word for "obstacle", "scandal"
means the "stone on which one stumbles";
yet Jesus has just told Peter:

>   **"You are Peter and on this rock I will build my church."**

Now he says,
>   **"You are a stone that makes me stumble."**

The stone on which the Church is to be built

can become the stone that makes people stumble and fall
if it does not reveal the true face of Jesus,
but seeks instead to conform to the ways of culture and of society.
Jesus adds:

> **"Your thoughts are not the thoughts of God but of human beings."**

How difficult it is to enter into God's vision of pain.
Our first reaction is like Peter's.
Pain frightens us
    and brings us back to the first pain of our childhood,
which is like a deep, open wound at the heart of our heart:
the pain of feeling rejected, unwanted, unloved, put aside.
Physical pain can be terrible but it is bearable
if there is someone with us who loves us and helps us,
and if we have the right medication.
The pain of not being loved, of being all alone, is unbearable
and makes everything else unbearable.
Our reaction to pain can be strong.
We can be angry with pain and with God.
Pain can be intolerable;
we see no meaning in it.

Jesus did not come into the world to explain suffering
nor to justify its existence.
He came to reveal that we can all alleviate pain,
through our competence and our compassion.
He came to show us that every pain, every hurt we experience
can become an offering,
and thus a source of life for others
in and through Jesus' offering of love to the Father.

Humanly speaking this all seems impossible and incomprehensible.
It is only in and through the grace of the Holy Spirit
that we can learn to make it an offering

and so begin to discover in this humble gift
a mystery of love and communion;
a mystery which gives life to the world.

The mystery of the cross

Let us look more closely at Peter
and try to understand his reaction
  to the weakness and fragility of Jesus,
so that we can better understand what happens in our own hearts
when we are faced with pain and with weakness.
In this way we shall discover more deeply the meaning of l'Arche.
L'Arche is founded on weakness and pain.
L'Arche was born
because the Luisitos, the Erics and the Claudias of our communities
were in pain and anguish;
it was founded as an answer to their cry of distress.
We in l'Arche cannot of course eliminate all the causes of pain and
    anguish in our people
but we can welcome some people;
we can love them and alleviate some of their pain.

If we welcome those who are in pain,
if we try to understand them and be with them,
their pain will become more bearable.
L'Arche is neither a school nor a hospital.
People go to the hospital to get better and then they leave.
They go to school to learn and then leave.
When we welcome people in l'Arche, they can stay
because l'Arche wants to be a family.

When we welcome people into our homes
because they are fragile, wounded, in anguish,
they may gradually become more peaceful and grow in trust
but they will never be fully healed.
Claudia will never be able to go to university!

Luisito will never be able to talk!
The fragility and disability of each one remains;
and as they grow older
    they will enter into other forms of weakness.

We are called to share our lives with people in pain,
to live a covenant with them.
We have all met people who have been wounded in life.
We have all been hurt at some point
    and at some place in our own lives.
We need to deepen our understanding of our reaction to pain
and reflect on that reaction.
How do we react when we are faced with our own pain
    and with the pain of others?

Peter could not stand pain.
When Jesus was arrested and led away to a mock trial,
Peter said three times:
"I do not know that man!"
Mathew even tells us that the third time Peter began to swear and
    to cry out:
"I do not know that man!"
Peter was not a man who was easily frightened.
He was courageous, always ready to fight for the one he loved;
he was ready to die for Jesus.
He had told Jesus, "I will give my life for you"
and yet later he says, "I do not know that man!"

Something has broken inside Peter and he starts to doubt.
Strangely enough, it is true: he does not know *this* man;
he does not recognise in this weak, battered person
the man who had spoken with authority,
    the man who had performed miracles
and called Peter to follow him.
Peter had been attracted and seduced by a powerful Jesus.
He had followed Jesus because of his power.

People can become Christians or join a group or a community
because they have had a strong experience,
witnessed a miracle
or have felt interiorly transformed.
But that is just the beginning.

Peter had witnessed the healings
the multiplication of bread
the transfiguration
the resurrection of Lazarus
and the fervour of the crowds.
He was fascinated by the freedom and the strength
    of Jesus' words;
the deep unity between what Jesus said and what he did;
by the newness of his message and the way it brought life to others.

Peter believed that Jesus was the Messiah
who would liberate Israel from the occupying Roman army
and give a new dignity, freedom and power to his people.
Peter had a dream of a messianic triumph
    and it was becoming a reality.
He would be on the "winning team".
Too often, we dream of being on the winning team
whether it be in sports, in politics, in community
    or even in Church.
We all want to be part of a group
that is on the "right side" and that will triumph over others.

Faced with the weakness and littleness of Jesus,
Peter does not and *cannot* understand.
The Holy Spirit has not yet revealed to him
that Jesus gives life – gives life to all humankind –
not only by his words, his acts and his miracles
but especially by the love of his heart
which brought him to give his life in sacrifice.

We all have to make the same journey as Peter
and so come to a greater understanding
that those who are blessed
are not those who succeed "religiously"
but those who keep trusting
    even as they live the experience of failure.
When we succeed in something, we naturally feel blessed.
But how can we feel blessed
    when we are put aside, disregarded, humiliated?
How can we discover that failure is not merely negative?
Are we not scandalised by the extreme "failure" of life
    which is death?
How can we understand that the one who is dying on the cross,
in poverty and rejection,
— the one who keeps on trusting in spite of rejection —
is indeed blessed by God?

How can we believe that there can be a meaning to failure?
How can we believe in the value of the lives
of Luisito, Lucien, Claudia and others
    we have welcomed into our homes;
those whose lives began as a failure?
Luisito, Lucien, Claudia and the others are weak in their minds and
    bodies.
They have lived the pain of rejection.
They will never know great success.
We can only welcome weakness and see value in it
if we ourselves grow in the belief
that Jesus "makes all things new".
There is such a need in all of us
to be identified with a strong, successful group.
We can welcome people who are weak and poor into l'Arche
and can still judge or be disappointed
when we discover the littleness and poverty
    of our own community.

Consciously or unconsciously
   we admire movements in the Church
that are "successful";
that attract great numbers and seem secure and strong.
We can distrust communities that are suffering.
We find it difficult to accept in all truth
   the essential message of Jesus:
the deep and intimate unity between the Cross and the
   Resurrection.
We have difficulty in trusting
when we (or our community) are in pain.
We may worship the cross of Jesus
but we have difficulty accepting it when it enters our own lives.

To be compassionate as Mary was compassionate

Peter cannot bear to see the weakness and pain of Jesus.
He runs away.
Mary remains with Jesus,
standing at the foot of the cross.

Mary's first perception of Jesus
   was not as a strong leader and prophet
but as a tiny baby in her womb;
then as a child in her arms,
a child who needed to be nourished, bathed and held,
a child who needed to be loved.
Like every other child, Jesus, God-made-flesh, needed to be loved,
so that his human heart could grow in love.
Mary was able to give him the unconditional love he needed
because she herself was "full of grace",
transparent with love, pure of heart.
She loved him out of the fullness of her heart,
and the grace within her,
not out of her own needs or inner void,
or because she had suffered a lack of love herself.

We often love others because we have an emptiness, an inner void,
a need that we are trying to fill.
We can try to possess those we love
   in our family, our community, our circle of friends.

Mary loved fully ... and truthfully ...
There was a wholeness about her.
Everything she did was for Jesus, not for herself.
She did not try to hurry through bathtimes, mealtimes or playtimes
so that she could go and pray
or do other "more important things".
All the daily tasks of her life
were a prayer,
her every gesture
a time of communion with Jesus,
because all was centred on Jesus.
It is important to take time
and to look quietly at Mary with Jesus.
We need to understand how all *our* gestures,
and even *our* physical bodies,
can become a source of life,
a presence of God,
a "sacrament".
A sacrament is a "sign", a place
that renders God present.
For Mary, the body of Jesus was a "sacrament",
   the place where she met God.

We often say therefore that the weak and the broken
   are a "sacrament"
which means that they render Jesus present:

> **"Whatever you did to the least of these, you did it to me."**
> (Matt 25:45)

When Mary held the child Jesus in her arms, she was holding God.
When Mary bathed the body of Jesus, she was caring for God.

As she touched the body of Jesus, she was touching God.
Her touch was a source of grace.

I understood a bit better the deep meaning of touch
when I held or bathed the little, wounded body of Eric
while I was living in the Forestière.
I used to speak to Eric,
but as he was both blind and deaf he was unable to hear me.
The only way he could sense my presence
was by the way I touched him.
Touch "spoke" to him.

We in l'Arche have become very sensitive to this mystery of the
   Body of Jesus,
because many of our people do not understand words.
We communicate God's love to them
   through the way we touch them and care for them.
We are learning how to touch the weak and the broken
with great respect, great tenderness
because their bodies are temples of the Holy Spirit.
They become "sacrament", a presence of God for us.
In communion with them,
we are in communion with Jesus.

Mary was not shocked by the weakness or littleness of God;
the tears and the cry of the child Jesus;
his needs, his hurts;
his anguish and agony.
Mary was at the cross
standing close to Jesus stripped and vulnerable,
in communion with her beloved son.

At the crucifixion Jesus suffered excruciating physical pain.
Those who were crucified were stretched out on the cross,
   hanging from their arms;
they could not breathe
   unless they were able to push up on their legs

and fill their lungs with a little air.
The bodies had to be taken down before the Sabbath.
For this reason, the Roman soldiers broke the legs of the crucified
    in order to kill them;
they could no longer push up to fill their lungs.
As Jesus was already dead, the gospel tells us that the soldiers did
    not break his legs,
but pierced his side with a spear.

Let us take time to look at Jesus on the cross,
to pray with him
and to enter into the mystery of his suffering and death.

Those who were crucified were stripped of their clothes
and of their dignity.
Jesus was naked.
His nakedness added to his humiliation.
His arms were stretched out on the cross.
For three long hours he had to struggle to push up on his legs,
in order to catch a breath;
his feet pierced by nails,
he could barely whisper.
Three long hours of anguish and agony.
His friends had all left him.
Peter had denied Jesus; saying that he did not know him.
The other disciples had lost confidence,
no longer believed in him or his mission from God.
What terrible pain!
A crowd, including some scribes and Pharisees,
    had gathered below the cross,
looking on, mocking him,
rejoicing in their "victory" over Jesus.

Mary remains standing silent, at the foot of the cross.
She hears the words that Jesus can barely utter:
    "Father, forgive them, for they do not know what they do."

At Cana Mary had heard Jesus say, "My hour has not yet come."
Now she knows that his hour has indeed come.
She trusts in Jesus and in the importance of the moment
and is reminded of the words of the prophet Isaiah ...

> no human beauty, a man of pain familiar with suffering ...
> and through his wounds we are healed. (cf. Is 53)

The great mystery of our Christian faith
is that we have been saved by a condemned man;
that we have been healed by his wounds.
Christ had to die in order to express his abundant love.
His suffering became a source of life for us all.

Mary is a strong and gentle presence; she is with Jesus.
She is not angry with the scribes and the Pharisees.
She is not afraid.
She is not disappointed.
Her whole being reaches out to Jesus
saying: "I trust you. I trust you."
Jesus has been stripped of all, has lost all,
but he lives this communion with Mary.
Jesus, the Word–made–flesh, came into the world
in communion with Mary
and he leaves this world
in communion with Mary.
And in this communion of their hearts,
she offers all to the Father.
The words of the old man, the prophet Simeon, are fulfilled:
her heart has been pierced by a sword (cf. Lk 2:25).

And this communion with Mary
    is all that Jesus has at this moment.
Yet he strips himself even of that bonding.
He looks at Mary and says:

"Woman, here is your son" (Jn 19:25)

and to the beloved disciple:

"Here is your mother."

As soon as he has given Mary to John
Jesus says, **"I thirst"**
which in biblical language often means "I am in anguish".
Then immediately afterwards he gives up the Spirit and dies.

Mary is teaching us something about compassion
which is so fundamental to our community life.
That is why Mary is so important for l'Arche.

Mary can teach us how to *be with* and *walk with*
    people who are in anguish;
people who will never be healed or cured.
We need the compassionate presence of Mary
    in our lives and in our communities
in order to be close to those in anguish,
and to share our lives with them.
Some people say that we are "wasting our time"
    by living with our people;
that we could have done something more "useful" with our lives.
They are convinced that the lives of our people
are insignificant and irrelevant;
that our life with them
is insignificant and irrelevant.
But to be with them in their pain,
to live in communion with them,
is the sign of our love.

The spirituality of l'Arche is deeply linked
    to the hidden life of Jesus
at Calvary, at Bethlehem and at Nazareth.

In his own pain and agony, Jesus helps us to grasp
the mystery of human pain;
the mystery of our own wounds, our fragility and our brokenness,
our fear of rejection or of having no place in society.
Our anguish and confusion can become a source of life
when united to Jesus on the cross and in the resurrection.

We do not need to live our entire life angry
    with our past or with our weakness.
We do not have to be resentful towards our parents,
    our society or our church
because they have hurt us.
We are called to discover that no pain is ever useless.
It is more like the manure spread on the ground.
It smells horrid and seems only to be waste,
but in fact it enriches and nourishes the earth,
allowing it to bring forth new life.
Nothing is lost.
Jesus welcomes everything that is broken.
If we give him our weakness
he will transform it into a source of life.

Jesus helps us to take our pain
and use it as an offering.
That does not mean that we should not do everything we can
    to alleviate it!
If someone has a toothache, we should take him to a dentist,
not just tell him that we love him!
Likewise, someone in mental anguish needs competent help.
When faced with pain and suffering,
we need to discover compassion based on competence.

But when a mother has just lost a child,
or a woman her husband,
or when a young man learns
    that he will never be able to walk again,

they need not only competent help
   but the presence of a compassionate person.
When people are in the last stages of illness
everything should be done to alleviate the pain
   and make them comfortable
but they need also the simple presence
   of someone who loves them.

In our l'Arche communities we need compassion
that is both competence and "presence".
We need to know how to alleviate pain
   and how to comfort people in pain.
But all the competence in the world
   will never eliminate all the pain,
heal all the anguish,
mend all those who are "broken" ...
We need to learn how to *be with* those in pain,
to remain close to them, like Mary.

With Mary we will discover the mystery of our own suffering,
and how to offer it up to God with her,
   in union with Jesus
in order to give life to the world.

DAY SIX

"Blessed are the gentle of heart ... "
(Matthew 5)

Learning how to wait in hope

The body of Jesus is taken down from the cross.
Mary holds her beloved son for the last time.
The following day, that we call "Holy Saturday",
   is a day of waiting and of hoping.
I always have the impression on Holy Saturday
   that the whole world waits.
Whether we want to admit it or not our whole lives are spent
   in waiting, in expectation,
even if we do not always know what we are waiting for.

Young people are waiting for the moment they will meet
the one who will love them "forever".
Many people are waiting for the day they will discover
   their vocation in life.
Couples are living in the expectation of a new baby.
Elderly people await the moment of death.
In one way or another we are all waiting, living in expectation.

People come to see me sometimes
   because they are in unbearable situations:
the young man caught up in alcohol who has tried everything to
   stop drinking,
but nothing seems to work;
the woman in anguish, desperately looking for help
and unable to find it;
the husband and wife who no longer get along,
who fight and hurt each other
and no matter how hard they try, nothing seems to change.
They do not know what to do or what to hope for –
a change? a miracle? a cure?
It is as if they are living and waiting without hope.

Once again Mary is our model.
After the crucifixion, she waited, not knowing what to expect,
but waiting in peace and in trust.
Jesus had said that in three days he would rise up.
She did not know what that meant.
Was he going to rise up as Lazarus rose up?

The disciples waited too, each in their own way.
It is not easy to learn how to wait.

Mary of Magdala waited impatiently.
Time weighed heavily on her.
She was desperate for the Sabbath Day to end
so that she could rush to the tomb!
She wanted to be close to the body of Jesus once again.
She wanted to see him rise up.
But how would he do this?
Finally, weeping and fearful, she ran to the tomb,
and found it empty.
She rushed for help.
Mary, the mother of Jesus, was not agitated;
she did not run to the tomb.
She waited for Jesus.
He had said he would rise up on the third day.
She trusted.
The disciples from Emmaus could not wait peacefully;
they fled back to their home town.
They couldn't stand the tense atmosphere, the anguish
after the death of Jesus;
the waiting, without knowing what was going to happen.

The other disciples reacted with disbelief
when the women came and told them
that Jesus had risen.
They thought that these women were hysterical
as they cried out in their excitement:

"He is alive!"
"We have seen him!"
Each one of us lives this anguish of waiting.
Very few of us know how to wait peacefully.
In times of confusion and conflict
    a whole community can split up;
members can leave.

How difficult it is to wait
when we are in pain and in anguish
and do not understand.
We try to force events, to do anything to distract ourselves.
We throw ourselves into hyperactivity or into any activity
that might ease the pain
or release the anguish that is gradually overwhelming us.
Or else we want to break with everything,
to try to escape and run away.
It is difficult to remain still
when nothing seems to be happening.
We have to learn how to wait patiently
    in times of pain and grief;
to wait in an attitude of prayer and offering.

Let us ask Jesus to teach us how to wait quietly,
often without understanding.
We human beings want to know, to understand and to move ahead
and that can be good;
we have minds that seek to understand.
However we have to accept sometimes
that there are things we cannot yet understand.

Mary and Joseph had lost the child Jesus
on their way back from the pilgrimage to Jerusalem.
For three days they looked for him.
Eventually, when they did find him, Jesus told them:

"Did you not know that I must be in my Father's house?"

(Lk 2:49)

And the gospel adds that Mary and Joseph did not understand
what he had said to them.

There are many things we do not understand.
We have to wait for the light to come.
We need to wait and pray
   and to be attentive to the "moment" of God.
Once we have done all that we can
we need to learn how to wait.

Mary is the one who can teach us how to wait
when we face the darkness, brokenness and fragility of our world,
when we face our own darkness, brokenness and fragility –
to wait ... trusting that new life will be given.

Our greatest, deepest yearning is for new life,
for a rebirth, a resurrection,
  at the time of our death and at the end of time;
but also at *this present moment ... today, now.*
We yearn to be freed from the prison of our fears,
from our sense of powerlessness,
from all that prevents us from being fully alive!
We have this deep desire to be fully alive!

The resurrection of Jesus was the most extraordinary cosmic event
   of all time
and yet it was an extraordinarily humble and hidden occurrence.
We need to look at the resurrection of Jesus
in order to comprehend the hidden mystery and humility
of our own resurrection.
We tend to look for God in spectacular events;
we do not always recognise God's presence in our lives,
when God comes humbly, simply, like a gentle breeze.

On that Easter morning,
Jesus did not rise up triumphantly over the temple of Jerusalem,
with the sound of trumpets and the clashing of cymbals,
in front of a great crowd.
He appeared to a few people, individually,
like the two disciples on their way to Emmaus.
He simply walked and talked with them.
Then, little by little, they recognised that it was Jesus
and that he had risen.

With their hearts full of joy,
   the two disciples rushed back to Jerusalem
to tell the others what had happened.

> While they were talking about this, Jesus stood among them
> and said to them: "Peace be with you."
> They were startled and terrified and thought that they were
> seeing a ghost. (Lk 24:36)

Their immediate reaction was one of fear ...
and yet they knew it was Jesus.
The women had told them that Jesus had risen.
Peter had seen the empty tomb.
The disciples of Emmaus had shared their experience
and yet the other disciples still did not believe.

> He said to them: "Why are you frightened
> and why do doubts arise in your hearts?
> Look at my hands and my feet; see that it is I myself.
> Touch me and see; for a ghost does not have flesh and bones
> as you see that I have." And when he had said this, he showed
> them his hands and his feet. (Lk 24:38–40)

Then come the extraordinary words:

> "while in their joy they were disbelieving and still
> wondering ..."

It shows the hidden mystery
  and the humility of Jesus' resurrection.
It all seemed so simple that the disciples had trouble believing it
  was true.
No cosmic illuminations, no earth-shattering revelations.

Jesus continued:

> **"Have you anything here to eat?"**
> **They gave him a piece of grilled fish**
> **and he took it and ate it in their presence.** (Lk 24:42-3)

We need to look at what *our* resurrection means
in the light of the resurrection of Jesus.
Does it mean that we are suddenly and completely changed?

We are truly men and women of resurrection
because that which we yearn for has already happened.
This new life, new birth, is given at baptism
when we are reborn in the Holy Spirit.
Yet it also remains so hidden and unassuming:
like a tiny seed
that grows and develops in the vulnerable earth of our being.

We are a wounded, broken people,
our reactions springing from fear and anguish.
Our vulnerable hearts are so frightened of pain and rejection
that we put up barriers.
But if we allow the Holy Spirit to enter into our hearts,
they will be changed and transformed, little by little,
through her presence.

Growing in trust

We all dream of having some kind of spectacular conversion,
in which everything in our lives suddenly changes completely ...
  and forever

– like Paul on the road to Damascus!
In fact we do not know how long Paul's conversion actually took,
nor how it was prepared,
nor what followed afterwards.
We are impatient and find it difficult to accept that
even after an important experience of the love of God
    or a deep conversion
we are still not perfect.
We may recognise the change within ourselves;
our eyes have been opened and we see things in a new light.
We may have found our way, our call,
but *everything* is not changed.
Shadow areas still exist;
some wounds and weaknesses are still there,
    still ready to react and cry out in anger.

We long for a big, final experience of change.
We forget that life is a question of gradual growth.
It takes nine months for a child to develop in his/her mother's
    womb.
Then there is the miracle of birth as the child pushes forth into the
    world.
Then there are the various stages of development that will take
    years:
the first smile, the first steps, studies, and so on.
Growth is an evolving process towards greater maturity
until we reach the phase of diminished abilities, and decline.
This is a time of greater maturation.
The growth that comes through decline
and the loss of our physical and intellectual capacities
are just as important as our earlier development.
Our experience of strength and well-being is short lived.
Each of us is destined for old age and decline.

I remember meeting Pedro Arrupé, a Spanish priest,
who was the "Father General" of the Jesuits for many years.

He was an extraordinary man, gifted in many languages,
and with an amazing vision
    for the world and for the Christian Church;
a man filled with life and joy.
When our community went on pilgrimage to Rome in 1980 we
    visited him.
He spent time with us and sang us a song in his native Basque.
His voice filled the whole room!
He was truly one of the great men of vision of the
    twentieth century.

I was even more touched the last time I visited him.
He had just suffered a stroke and could no longer speak or read.
I offered him a book *I Meet Jesus*,
    with drawings, designed for children.
He looked at the pictures
    and his eyes shone like the eyes of a child.
He lived for another ten years, growing weaker,
    becoming incontinent and needing to be fed and bathed,
    unable to do anything unaided.

For each of us, our lives are leading to that same weakness and
    decline.
We will not all live and die as Pedro Arrupé lived and died
but sooner or later we will all grow older, weaker
    and more vulnerable.
We need to learn how to accept that fragility,
and how to enter into the mystery of growth through weakness.

My own mother lived to be nearly ninety-three.
As she grew older, she became weaker, had trouble walking
and could not dress herself.
She could no longer read and gradually became blind
but she continued to grow in her acceptance of reality,
    despite her decline.
To grow in maturity is to grow in this acceptance of reality;

no longer to take refuge in illusions.
It is to give thanks for what we *have*
instead of weeping over what we *have not*.

However, we never really come to full maturity.
We are all struggling with reality in one way or another,
with the way we are living at a given moment
or with what we have known from the past ...
So much of our energy is taken up in fighting reality
because we want it to be otherwise,
we want to live in the past or we project too much into the future.

It is the same story for all of us.
As children in school we say:
"I'll be happy as soon as I am old enough to get out of school and
    can work!"
Once out of school and with a job, we say:
"Ah, I can't wait until I get married, then I will be happy!"
A while after the wedding celebration,
when the couple realises that life is a bit lacking in variety,
they say, "But when we have our own children ... then we will be
    really happy."
Once the children are there, it's wonderful,
    but they cry in the night
and we sigh, "Ah, when the children get older ... "
Then when the children do grow up and create all kinds of
    problems,
the couple dreams of the children leaving home and they will
    finally be alone.
As the couple grows old, they think of the past and say:
"Wasn't it wonderful in the good old days, when we were
    younger!!"

We have difficulty living the present moment,
trusting in the presence of God in the here and now
and giving thanks.

Yet that is precisely where the mystery of the Incarnation lies;
the revelation that God is hidden in reality.
God is not someone inaccessible, "out there" in the sky,
out of the reach of human beings.
We do not have to search for God "out there" or in the future.
God is close to us, present to us —
eternally present in the "now" of each moment.
God is in the eternal here and now,
even in our brokenness and woundedness.
The life of each one of us is a story of growth
towards a greater openness and inner freedom
towards a greater acceptance of reality,
the reality of our own story
and the truth of who we are and who others are.
It is a long journey.

As people grow older and as their strength diminishes
they often become more accepting of their lives and of reality.
However, old age can make some people bitter and desperate;
they become angry with life, with themselves, with their weakness
and with the awareness of the nearness of death and the end of
their lives.
It takes time to learn to embrace reality
to enter into a "bonding" with reality;
a bonding with our own weakness and poverty.
We need to spend time with Jesus to give thanks.
We are often like the "bakouris",
beautiful trees in the Amazon that grow very slowly.
It takes forty years for them to bear fruit!
We too have to wait sometimes thirty or forty years before we see
the fruits of our lives!
Yet we are called to trust that the fruits are there,
quietly being prepared in the secret of our being.
We have to learn how to wait for God's time,
to live in God's time.
There is *our* time and there is *God's* time.

God is patient and knows how to wait for us.
We have to learn to be patient and to wait for God.

The mystery of Christianity lies in humility:
the humility of God
and in the humble acceptance of this humble God
who comes to us in our reality *today*.
Each one of us lives
   a strange and mysterious partnership with God.
Each one is called to walk step by step, with Jesus
learning to walk to the same rhythm as Jesus –
I would even say learning to "dance" to the same rhythm as Jesus.

Jesus gives us the grace we need
but it is up to us to take the necessary steps
to nourish this covenant relationship.
God never forces us or manipulates us.
When I listen to people and accompany them
   on their inner journey,
I am touched by God's gentleness, humility,
and deep respect for each one,
   for who they are and where they are on their journey.

Jesus called the rich young man and said to him:

> **"Only one thing is lacking.**
> **Go, sell what you have, give your money to the poor**
> **and come and follow me."** (Mk 10:21)

The young man could not do it.
Jesus did not insist.
He did not run after him trying to seduce him or convince him
promising to give him riches and power.

God respects our freedom
and does not use publicity or slogans.

God loves us too much to treat us in that way.
That is God's weakness.
Jesus says to each one of us ... *"If you want*, come,
but I am not forcing you to do so ...
I cannot promise you success in this world
but I promise to *be with you always*.
We will walk together."
Jesus will never leave us,
even if we make mistakes, fall into depression or turn away from him.
Jesus will wait for us to return.
We human beings tend to "use" other people
     for our own interests, our own purposes.
If they do not correspond to our expectations
or are no longer "useful"
we leave them.

Jesus does not turn anyone away
and does not turn away from anyone.
He waits with love.
All he wants is that we grow in inner freedom
and that we love more fully and freely.
And this can take time.
But that is the humility of the resurrection –
the littleness of our growth in the Holy Spirit.

It is also part of the humility and poverty of l'Arche.
We need good assistants in our houses.
Sometimes they come
and sometimes there is a shortage of assistants.
It is the humility and poverty of our Luisitos and Claudias.
They are always there in the community
and they invite assistants to stay on with them
but they never judge or condemn assistants when they leave.
In l'Arche we need to be men and women of patience.
We need to grow and trust in the certitude
that Jesus is walking with us.

Jesus wants us to take good care of ourselves,
to be well physically and spiritually,
to take the necessary rest and the proper food,
to find the right spiritual nourishment.
Jesus wants us to place at his feet all that we are carrying in our hearts
and to rest quietly with him;
trusting that we are gradually growing in his love.

If we listen to the word of God,
if we take God's promises seriously,
if we are nourished by the liturgy and the sacraments,
if we worship regularly with others in church,
if we accept to be accompanied on our life's journey
    by a man or woman of God,
if we walk simply and humbly with the weak and the poor,
we will begin, little by little, to understand things
    we have never before understood.
We will become more peaceful, more loving.

God is leading us gently and quietly,
for God is Love.
God is total gift of self.
God is abundant in his giving.
His greatest desire is to give himself to us
in this life-giving covenant relationship
so that we might be men and women fully alive.

We need to become friends of time
and to accept that growth takes time.
We need to be men and women who know how to wait
because we know that the Eternal One,
who is beyond all limited time,
is also present in every moment of the day;
we need to know that we are called to live and walk with God
    today
and every day, day after day.

To open up to tenderness

Helen, who has now died, was fifteen years old
  when she was welcomed into the l'Arche community, "Punla",
  in the Philippines.
Up to that time, Helen had spent her whole life in a hospital.
She was blind, unable to walk, to talk or to use her hands.
Communication was difficult.
When I visited "Punla", Keiko, who cared for Helen,
  told me how difficult it was to live with her.
There was no reaction, no emotion;
all she could do was open her mouth for the baby feeding bottle.
I encouraged Keiko to continue to gently spend time with Helen,
talking with her, touching her and holding her tenderly.
I told her that, God willing, Helen might one day smile
and on that day maybe Keiko could send me a postcard.
Months later I received a card from Manila:
"Helen smiled today."
She had found new life;
a trickle of new life had opened up and flowed forth in her.
She had begun to trust.

Human beings are made for communion.
If there is no communion, we close up on ourselves;
we are unable to communicate; to enter into the flow of life.
It is as if there is no irrigation, no circulation of life.
A child abandoned at birth closes up in sadness and depression
and becomes incapable of reacting or communicating.
For a child, this communion is vital, the to and fro of love,
wherein each one gives and receives.
Sometimes I hear psychologists say that children
  are incapable of loving
and that love only grows and deepens later
as we grow in our gift of self
and become more generous and more altruistic.
But little children do love,

though not with a love that is generosity,
only with a love that is trust,
  a love which is a communion of hearts.
Trust is already a gift of self.
We adults have often grown in generosity
but have lost this basic trust —
a trust in God,
a trust in others,
a trust in ourselves.
We have been hurt or manipulated in the past
and are afraid of being hurt again
if we put too much trust in others.
Instead we develop our defence mechanisms
and become independent and self-sufficient.
Children are not self-sufficient.
They need others to cover them up at night if they are cold.
They are dependent on others for everything
and can only cry out in their need.
Their cry is in itself a sign of trust;
trust that someone will come and answer their cry,
that someone is there who wants them to be well and happy.

When a mother hears her child's cry
  she knows how to interpret it,
— whether it is a sign that he is hungry or frightened or in pain —
because she loves and knows her child.
We in l'Arche have to learn how to interpret the cry of our people
especially when they are non verbal;
their only language is their facial expression, their gesture
or sometimes their violence.
We need to understand what they are asking for,
what they are refusing,
and where there is pain.

The language of adolescents also needs to be understood
  and respected.
Even though they may have a greater capacity for words

they cannot always put the right words
on what they are living and wanting to say;
so they often express themselves through their gestures
    and attitudes.
In fact this is true of us all:
so often we do not know how to express the hurt or anguish we
    are feeling;
we need the help of someone who can understand and interpret
    our cry.

Children may not always understand a lot of words
but they can sense whether or not people are happy that they exist,
that they are important, loved and respected;
they sense it through the way they are touched, bathed, fed
    and by the tone of voice.
In the same way, when we speak,
the tone of our voice says more than our words.
When ministers and priests preach,
the tone of their voice says more than their words
and shows whether they are speaking from a personal relationship
    with Jesus or not.
Just the way we say the name "Jesus" can show our love –
    or lack of it –
and the quality of our relationship of trust in Jesus.
It is painful to sense the gap between what we are saying
    and what we are living.

A child senses whether he/she is important for the other,
whether he/she is loved or not.
During one of my visits to Canada I visited a children's hospital
where the nurses working with children with disabilities had their
    eyes glued to the television while they were changing the
    children's diapers.
Have you ever tried to hold a conversation with someone
while they are watching television?

We do not know Helen's whole story,
   all that she lived in the Philippines,
but we do know that she must have been terribly hurt.
At some moment she must have called out for love and tenderness,
needed to know that she was unique and important for someone
but no one answered that cry.
So one day she stopped calling out
and just closed up in herself
and withdrew from the world around her.
We all do that when people hurt us,
we close up within ourselves.
But we at least can do things to get out of ourselves
we can clean the house, go to the movies, etc.
Helen could not.
How could Helen move out of her prison of fear and despair,
open up and communicate once again with others?
Only by meeting someone whom she trusted,
who would not judge her, condemn her or leave her.

I told the story of Helen to a group of young people in difficulty
and I asked them if there was someone they could talk to
when they were feeling hurt or guilty,
when they felt violent or suicidal.
I did not expect any answer from them
but I could tell from the look on their faces
that many did not have anyone to turn to.

How was it possible to be close to Helen and to reassure her?
Her whole being was crying out for love and acceptance
but this cry was locked up inside her.
Keiko admitted that it was hard to be with Helen
because her total lack of reaction
reminded Keiko of her own fears and anguish.
Whenever Keiko was especially tired,
feelings of anger and depression could rise up in her
and she would lose patience.

So many times she felt like crying out:
    "Why don't you respond?
    I wash you, clothe you, feed you;
    carry you gently and walk with you,
    why doesn't that seem to matter to you?
    Does it make sense to spend my life with you?
    Is it just a waste of time?
    I can't go on like this!"

When people do not respond in the way we want or expect,
we can become anguished and angry
even if we hide all that under a mask of politeness.
Silence can be filled with tenderness
but also with hatred.
We can be depressed but continue to smile.
Clowns make people laugh
even though they themselves may be crying inside.

Helen's story in l'Arche was brief.
"Helen came, she smiled, she was baptised and then she died."
Her death was painful: she had an epileptic fit and choked to death.
But as her community leader said,
"We are sure she is watching over the community now
    like a guardian angel."
Her brief stay in our community – less than a year –
was perhaps just the time she needed
    in order to learn how to smile –
the time she needed to teach us about the secret
    of the communion of hearts.

Helen lived only for communion.
She had the time to discover communion
and to show us how frightened we can be of communion,
how we too set up defence mechanisms.
We are not immobile like Helen
but sometimes our hyperactivity can be a way of hiding ourselves
    from others.

In order to be with people like Helen
we have to let go of *doing things*
and be open to simply *being with them.*
We have to be in touch with ourselves and at peace with ourselves;
in touch with the gentleness and tenderness
   in the depths of our hearts.

Helen lived the first beatitude: "Blessed are the poor ... "
she was so poor in every way.
She needed people around her who were living the beatitude:
"Blessed are the gentle of heart ... "
The more a person has been hurt
the more he or she needs a gentle presence and tender, loving care.
Bathing a dying person requires a great deal of tenderness,
a gentleness of both heart and body.
Helen taught us gentleness and tenderness.

CONCLUSION: *The one who answers the cry*

The mystery of l'Arche is a mystery of personal relationships:
covenant relationships between people who are very different;
the mysterious bonding between Keiko and Helen.
We become more aware that this bonding comes from God;
we yearn to be faithful to that covenant,
to take the downward path of the beatitudes
seeking to respect, understand and love others,
never using them to fill our own needs and our own emptiness.

But how quickly we can fall into routine
and get tired of being with others,
or enter the vicious circle of depression and aggression.
We can even become angry with ourselves
because we feel unable to be gentle and to accept others as they are,
unable to accept ourselves as we are.
We need to learn to be gentle with ourselves
as well as with the Helens.
We too have been hurt and cry out our pain,
our disappointments,
our incapacity to relate,
our aggressiveness and anger.
We can cry out as if in a void
or we can cry out to God.

In John's Gospel Jesus promises us:

> "I shall ask the Father
> and he will give you another Paraclete
> to be with you for ever ... " (14:16)

And he adds: "I shall not leave you orphans ... " (14:18)

Sometimes we translate the word "Paraclete" as "Comforter",
"Consoler", "Advocate"
but none of those words give the full meaning of this word.
Paracleitos comes from two Greek words:
para "close to" and *kaleo* "to call".
The verb *para-kaleo* means "to call out to someone for help".
The noun *paracleitos* means literally
  the "one who answers the call".

A mother is a "paraclete" for her child, a nurse for her patients.
Keiko and the community in Manila were a paraclete for Helen.
God is a Paraclete for each one of us,
the One who answers our call,
who knows how to interpret our cry,
who can draw us out of our inner prison of fear
and away from our defence mechanisms.
God is meek and gentle of heart
so that we need not be frightened to open up.

The most fundamental cry of the human being is "Mummy"
whether it comes from the child,
the dying person,
or the frightened man on the battlefield.
Our fundamental call is for the tenderness, gentleness
  and security of the mother.
Only a mother knows how to bend down and pick up
the fragile, hurt body of her little child.
Only a mother knows how to carry and care for him/her;
how to receive quietly and wipe away the tears.
Only a motherly love knows how to hold another
  in all their littleness and weakness
in a way that shows that they are loved:
– be it the littleness of a child or of a sick and dying person.

Only God can answer fully our cry for communion
and call us to live in communion with one another.
For even though we thirst for this communion with another,
we fear this bonding
because we are frightened of being hurt again.
We never fully realise the extraordinary gentleness, quiet presence
    of the Holy Spirit
who does not judge or condemn,
but knows our pain and our fears.
It was only the Holy Spirit
    who could unite Keiko and Helen in such a way.
Sometimes we can be generous –
write a cheque, give a gift, do a good deed for someone –
and then leave.
It is only through a gift of the Holy Spirit
that we can allow ourselves to become open and vulnerable
and can be faithful to a communion of hearts with another.

As we grow in our awareness of covenant as a gift of God,
let us give thanks for l'Arche
and let us celebrate this covenant.

In Trosly, after the community Eucharist on Holy Thursday,
we all return to our homes where we wash one another's feet
as Jesus asked us.
Then we share a meal, the pascal lamb, and we tell our stories.
Each one remembers what he/she has lived:
        "Where were you ten years ago?"
        "In a psychiatric hospital."
        "And you?"
        "I was alone, and very anguished."
        "And now we have been called together by God."
We give thanks that we are no longer alone,
that we have been called together, as brothers and sisters,
a beloved people of God,
    walking together with God.

CONCLUSION

That is the gift – and the miracle!

We have made the journey from the pain of loneliness
to the joy of community.
We have crossed over the "Red Sea"
from slavery and fear
to the promised land of communion.
It is good to celebrate this communion of hearts, this covenant
in our families and in our communities,
to give thanks for being called together;
it is good to rejoice in the reality that God has united us,
given us to each other.
And the weakest and most helpless are at the heart of everything
calling us to tenderness,
calling us to walk on the path of the beatitudes.

In the midst of our broken world
our communities and our families are called to become
      like small oases,
humble places of love
where we try to live covenant
between us
and in solidarity with the weak and the suffering
      throughout the world.
Our communities are not cut off from the world.
They are open to others in the local community
      and neighbourhood,
as well as to those who are far away.
We are all part of one and the same body,
each one of us, in his/her own way,
breathing the same breath of the Spirit of God.

In the Book of Isaiah, God says:

> **Is not this the sort of fast that pleases me:**
> **to break unjust fetters**

to undo thongs of the yoke
to let the oppressed go free
and to break all yokes?
Is it not sharing your food with the hungry,
and sheltering the homeless poor
(to share your life with the Luisitos and the Claudias and
the Helens);
if you see someone lacking clothes, to clothe them
and not turn away from your own kin?
Then your light will blaze out like the dawn
and your wound be quickly healed over.
Saving justice will go ahead of you
and Yahweh's glory come behind you.
Then you will cry out for help
and Yahweh will answer
(you will touch your own limits and insecurity and cry
out).
You will call and he will say, "I am here."
If you do away with the yoke, the clenched fist and malicious
words,
if you deprive yourself for the hungry
and satisfy the needs of the afflicted,
your light will rise in the darkness
and your darkest hour will be like noon.
Yahweh will guide you continually,
and will satisfy your needs in the scorched land;
he will give strength to your bones
(he will give the nourishment and energy you need)
and you will be like a watered garden,
like a flowing spring
whose waters never run dry. (Is 58:6–11)

I am convinced that God is watching over us,
watching over each and every one of our houses and communities.
God is calling us to be a source of unity in a divided world.
Wherever we may be, God is calling us

to be present to those in pain
– not to flee into dreams or illusions or theories.
God is calling us
to enter into the mud of reality,
the brokenness of people
and to discover that water springs from the mud of the earth
and from the reality of pain and weakness
in which we find God.

God, in Jesus, became flesh,
took on our humanity,
became matter
and entered into the world of movement and change;
into the world of pain.
We do not have to be frightened:
God is present with us,
in the Word,
in the community of believers,
in the Eucharist,
in the sacrament of forgiveness,
in the sacrament of the weak and the broken.
God is present – though hidden –
within our own being, in all our fragility.

With Mary, who carried within her
the hidden body of Jesus,
we can sing:

> "The Almighty One has done great things for me, and holy is his name.
> His mercy is for those who fear him, from generation to generation.
> He has shown strength with his arm;
> he has scattered the proud in the thoughts of their hearts.
> He has brought down the powerful from their thrones
> and lifted up the lowly;

he has filled the hungry with good things,
and sent the rich away empty.
He has helped his servant Israel in remembrance of his mercy
according to the promise made to our ancestors, to Abraham
and to his descendants forever." (Lk 1:46–55)